COMFORT ZONES

Women writers tackling
unfamiliar ground

—

An anthology in aid of
Women for Women International

Edited by Sonder & Tell

J I G S A W

First published in 2019 by

J I G S A W

001

This selection copyright
© Sonder & Tell, 2019

Text copyright © Alice-Azania Jarvis, Ana Santi, Anna Jones,
Ariane Sherine, Brita Fernandez Schmidt, Charlie Brinkhurst-
Cuff, Daisy Buchanan, Emma Gannon, Elizabeth Day, Farrah
Storr, Funmi Fetto, Gillian Orr, Irenosen Okojie, Lindsey
Hilsum, Marianne Power, Mina Holland, Natasha Lunn,
Nellie Eden, Olivia Sudjic, Pandora Sykes, Phoebe Lovatt,
Poorna Bell, Sophie Mackintosh, Sophie Wilkinson, Tahmina
Begum, Vicky Spratt, Yomi Adegoke, Zing Tsjeng

The moral right of the contributors has been asserted.

Text and cover design by
Duzi Studio

Printed and bound by CPI Group (UK) Ltd,
Croydon, CRO 4YY

A CIP record for this book is available
from the British Library

ISBN 978–1–527–23447–5

All correspondence to: Jigsaw,
159 Mortlake Road, Kew, Surrey, TW9 4AW

Women for Women International
is a registered charity: 1115109

For the women supported by
Women for Women International,
whose bravery has inspired this collection.

An Introduction by Sonder & Tell 1

LEARNINGS

Elizabeth Day
Things I Wish I'd Known About Success at 16 7

Ariane Sherine *On Being Enough* 12

Phoebe Lovatt *Slowing Down* 16

Poorna Bell *The Art of Being Alone* 20

Emma Gannon *29 Things I've Learned at 29* 25

Marianne Power *Why I Want to Be Rich* 30

Daisy Buchanan *On Toughening Up* 34

Funmi Fetto *Onijogbon and the Voice* 38

Farrah Storr *A Letter to My Timid Self* 43

RELATIONSHIPS

Alice-Azania Jarvis *Conversations with My Mother* 51

Lindsey Hilsum *Dear Marie* 58

Mina Holland *On My Parents* 63

Natasha Lunn *The Discomfort of Intimacy* 68

Pandora Sykes *Books for My Daughter* 73

Gillian Orr *On Turning Into Your Mother*   78

Nellie Eden *Typical Girls*   81

Anna Jones *On Motherhood*   86

WORKS OF FICTION

Yomi Adegoke *September Babies*   93

Ana Santi *The List*   99

Olivia Sudjic *Soft Hair*   103

Sophie Wilkinson
Ogres & Good Guys: A Story for My Nephews   109

NEW GROUND & BIG IDEAS

Irenosen Okojie *Nocturnal Zones and Dissident Women*   119

Zing Tsjeng *Comfort Food*   124

Vicky Spratt *Dare to Do*   129

Sophie Mackintosh *Attempts at Domesticity*   135

Charlie Brinkhurst-Cuff *On Narcissism*   140

Tahmina Begum *The Beauty of Sitting Still*   145

Brita Fernandez Schmidt *Afterword*   150

Jigsaw *A Note From The Publisher*   154

AN INTRODUCTION

By Sonder & Tell

All around us, there are products and services designed to engineer comfort. You can order a pizza to your door without getting out of your pyjamas, use an app to skim that long-winded non-fiction book. And what is the athleisure trend – which sanctions wearing tracksuits to work – other than a response to our desire for maximum ease?

Don't get us wrong: we all seek comfort. There's a reason why at our lowest ebb it's our closest friends we turn to, our mother's recipes we crave, elastic waistbands chosen over constricting jeans. In uncertain times, we all search for ways to make life lighter to lead.

But there is an insidious side to comfort. A kind of cotton wool which shields us from struggle and failure, from difference and difficulty. It's this sort of comfort that sees us accepting a run-of-the-mill salary when we know we're worth more, settling for a relationship that has clearly run its course, creating online worlds where the only opinions we hear are those that reinforce our own views. When we refuse to get off the island and out of the bubble, we fail to grow.

An exploration of discomfort is at the heart of this collection of essays, letters and stories. Our central question is: what happens when you ask women writers to abandon the themes and forms of writing that feel safe to them and to tackle something brave and new?

Within the pages of Comfort Zones you'll find a record of profound experience and experimental styles. We've asked writers to think about their usual subject matter, and then work against it. There are journalists tackling their first works of fiction, reflective essays that take an unflinching look at past failures, and big ideas for creating a kinder world. Behind the scenes, the British fashion brand Jigsaw has made a bold step in becoming a publisher, addressing its audience through stories rather than clothes. Meanwhile we – Sonder & Tell – have pulled together our first ever book over a period of just six months (as a benchmark, the publishing industry standard is about two years). What's the saying, again? A ship is safe in harbour, but that's not what ships are for.

The concept of comfort zones – of questioning the parameters we set ourselves and how it feels to move beyond them – has been inspired by the incredible stories of Women for Women International. Almost half a million survivors of war have taken part in their year-long training programmes in Afghanistan, Bosnia and Herzegovina, the Democratic Republic of the Congo, Iraq, Kosovo, Nigeria, Rwanda and South Sudan. Each woman, joining a group with 24 others, learns marketable job skills – such as tailoring, bread-making or poultry-keeping – so they can go on to earn a sustainable income. "The classes really made me brave – they pulled out the best from us," said Sylhane from Kosovo, who was able to use the funds from her small business to send her three children to school.

It is not our intention to draw parallels between women like Sylhane and the writers in this collection. Of course the bravery of completely rebuilding a life cannot be matched. Even the idea of having a comfort zone – a space where you feel safe – implies a certain privilege. You can't reach beyond what's comfortable if every day is a struggle for survival. That kind of ambition is a luxury reserved for the secure.

The aim of this anthology is to explore the idea of pushing boundaries – both big and small – as a means of expressing our deep respect for those supported by Women for Women International. We're grateful to all the contributors who have so generously joined us in donating time and skills to bring the project to life, so that 100% of the proceeds from this book can go towards furthering the charity's work.

This book elevates the concept of comfort zones – from a personal exploration of ease and discomfort to a communal conversation about the limits we set for ourselves as women. And through this dialogue, uncomfortableness actually starts to feel quite comfortable, collectively (how's that for an uncomfortable sentence?). We hope you feel inspired by the writings here and ready for the next challenge, whatever that might look like to you.

– Kate Hamilton and Emily Ames, Sonder & Tell

Sonder & Tell is a storytelling agency which helps brands develop a wider positive culture. Working with writers from their community, they dreamed up this book in support of Women for Women International, and then worked hand-in-hand with the fashion brand Jigsaw to bring it to life.

Elizabeth Day
Ariane Sherine
Phoebe Lovatt
Poorna Bell
Emma Gannon
Marianne Power
Daisy Buchanan
Funmi Fetto
Farrah Storr

LEARNINGS

THINGS I WISH I'D KNOWN ABOUT SUCCESS AT 16

Elizabeth Day

Elizabeth Day is a journalist, novelist and host of the podcast How to Fail with Elizabeth Day. She's used to talking about failure (and has a book published on the subject) but is rarely found talking directly about its counterpoint, success. Here, she tackles it head on.

Success will not always feel like success. A lot of the time it will feel like failure, like a challenge that needs to be overcome or a sludgy patch of ground that needs to be trudged through. Keep going and remind yourself that success can only truly be felt if you have its opposite for comparison.

Success isn't what the movies make it out to be. It's not a glorious montage of uncorked Champagne and dollar bills thrown into the air and scattered like confetti. It's not limousines or red carpets or famous friends or an aeroplane seat that reclines all the way back. True success is how you feel. It's looking yourself in the eye and knowing you're the person you want to be. It's about honouring that authenticity and being empowered by it. It's about knowing what has real value to you, as opposed to what other people think.

If you live your life according to what other people think, you're not living your life. You're trying to live theirs.

It's OK to make mistakes. It's not OK to ignore the lesson they're teaching you.

If you're successful, in whatever field you choose, you will attract criticism as well as praise. Remind yourself that you have no control over what other people think; that their opinions are formed from their own back catalogue of experiences; that what they say has more bearing on who they are than on who you are.

If you're provoking discussion then you're doing something right. If you're doing something you believe in, it's always better to make an impact than to disappear without trace.

Success is mistrusted in women. That's because we're not used to it. Successful women contradict the millennia of patriarchal conditioning that has convinced us men are the ones who deserve the garlands. This is not true. To show that it's not true through the things you do and achieve is a revolutionary act.

People say money doesn't change you. It does. Make sure it changes you for the better by not valuing it in and of itself, but for the things it can do and the lives it can alter.

Always be nice to someone asking for advice, and remember what it felt like when you were the one asking.

Every time you achieve something that comes with monetary reward, spend a portion of it on something tangible. A coat. A painting. A teapot. Something that you can look at or wear or hold to remind you: Yes, I did that. I earned this. Cherish those moments. They are fleeting, but they are important.

Life won't turn out how you expect. Good will always come from this, even if it doesn't feel like it at the time.

Ignore careers advisers. Ignore that weird test you did at school that told you you're destined to be a building society adviser. It turns out talent isn't measured by writing as many inverted Ss as you can in one minute.

Follow your instincts and listen to your gut. When things aren't a success, it's generally because you've been trying to create a narrative of what you hope is going on, rather than honestly evaluating the facts. Your mind is brilliant at telling stories. This is a blessing and, very occasionally, a curse.

You exist separately from your thoughts. You don't even need to try to be you. Once you realise this, it's the ultimate liberation.

Success in an intimate relationship depends on your being able to be yourself, at all times, and feeling good about that. Being yourself includes talking openly about the things you want. You should never be scared to do this. If you are scared or anxious – and your voice gets lost – then you need to end that relationship.

When a relationship finishes, it's a gift. As devastating as it feels, if a relationship ends it's always because it's not the right one for you. Give your heart six weeks to recover and do not judge yourself during this period of grief. This is what it is: grief. Drink, smoke, do whatever you have to do, and I promise that after six weeks, the pain will have lessened enough to live with.

You'll be surprised by how strong your heart is.

Better love is out there for you. If you're not used to being loved in the right way, this love will seem unfamiliar when it comes to you. You will question it. Ask yourself: does this person make me feel safe? If the answer is yes, sit with it for a bit. See how it settles. It might be the most beautiful love you've ever experienced. It might not arrive accompanied by fireworks.

Emotional resilience is like a muscle. It needs to be flexed.

Divide your work according to the three Ps: passion, prestige, pay. Whatever you take on, ask yourself if it's fulfilling one of those criteria. Only say yes if you're doing it because you love it (passion), because it's good for your reputation or brand (prestige) or because it's good money (pay). If the project in question isn't ticking any of those boxes, then say no.

Saying no is the ultimate power. It does not mean you will get less work. It means you're highly sought-after and that you know your own worth and people will want you more.

Always ask for a fee. But don't take the piss. If you're embarrassed about asking, know there are other people who aren't and they're almost certainly getting paid more than you.

If all else fails, take a gamble on yourself. It reaps the highest rewards.

Self-belief is the most powerful thing you can own.

ON BEING ENOUGH

Ariane Sherine

Ariane Sherine is a comedy writer, journalist, campaigner, musical comedian and author. She's chosen to write about her fear of not being 'young' anymore; of feeling as though time is running out to achieve everything she wants.

I am 38, and you heard it here first: I am old. The source of this information is my seven-year-old daughter. It's an unreliable testimony, you might argue, but in a way she's right: statistically, give or take a few years, I'm probably halfway through my life.

The thought makes me melancholic. Aged 19, I wanted to do so much: be an international pop star (it never happened, save for a song about my vagina on YouTube); get married (I did, but only for a year, and am now divorced and single); have a brood of kids I could mother tenderly and who would make the house noisy and joyful (I have one amazing girl, and wish I could clone her tenfold). I wanted to be a bestselling novelist (it's yet to happen); to have hundreds of close friends (I have two); and be invited to countless fabulous parties (please furnish my inbox if you're throwing one). And I yearned to be forever slim and pretty, instead of ending up obese with a chin full of stubborn hairs, which I pull out with tweezers during bathroom breaks at work.

Why do we women – instead of rejoicing in our successes – set ourselves such unattainable goals? Why do we always look to the unreachable, instead of looking at how far we've come? Why berate ourselves for not sailing among the stars, when we're improving things down on the ground? Men don't seem to obsess about this in the same way. It's madness, and it doesn't seem to stop however much we accomplish.

By anybody's standards, I'm an overachiever. I've dealt with an abusive childhood, domestic violence during pregnancy and years of struggling with poor mental health – all in order to create a beautiful life. I've starved myself, self-harmed, made two suicide attempts and experienced so much suicidal ideation I could easily have ended up dead. Instead, I enjoy a loving relationship with my adorable daughter, own a house straight out of Elle Decoration, write well-received books for a major publisher and hold down a full-time writing job. I've been lucky enough to work with many celebrities, was recently profiled in The Times, and my writing has been published in pretty much every UK newspaper. And I'm still two years off 40.

But still, like so many women, I tend to focus on the negatives instead of counting my blessings. To put into perspective how lucky I am, I just entered my net salary into globalrichlist.net to discover that I fall within the richest 0.29% of the world's population. The site tells me I make £20.83 an hour after tax, while an Ethiopian factory worker typically makes 15p. And yet, before this discovery, I felt sad that I wasn't in the top 0.01% and couldn't afford a £2m house in north London. I'm ashamed of myself, but shame won't help matters.

So, what will? Perhaps cutting ourselves some slack as women, acknowledging that we are under scrutiny from society and the media in a way that men aren't, at least not when it comes to physical appearance, family, marriage and parenting. This has a knock-on effect on our psyches. Perhaps happiness means cherishing what we have and accepting what we don't.

That doesn't mean we have to free ourselves of ambition entirely – we can still strive for more – but it means prioritising our own peace of mind above the need to tick off everything in our bullet journals. It means being glad our incredible bodies are keeping us alive, instead of hating them for their myriad imperfections. And it means an end to the endless comparisons: you and I are never going to be as accomplished as Michelle Obama (unless you're reading this, Michelle). And you know what? That's OK.

As for my beautiful, cheeky, funny seven-year-old: yes, darling, I'm old, at least in your eyes. And I've achieved so much, not least giving birth to you, a kind-hearted and affectionate daughter.

And I wish for you the same thing as all girls reading this: a life full of happiness and self-belief, in which you realise you are good enough, just as you are.

SLOWING DOWN

Phoebe Lovatt

*Phoebe Lovatt is a writer, moderator and founder of
The WW Club, a platform originally conceived to support
creative women but which has evolved into a resource for
independently minded professionals. Phoebe advises people to be
kind to themselves at work, but finds it tough to do that herself.*

There's a quote I used to think about a lot: "If everything seems under control, you're just not going fast enough." I'm not sure where I first read it – it was said by the Formula One racing driver Mario Andretti, about whom I know absolutely nothing else – but it stuck with me, becoming a mantra I repeated until it left deep grooves in my mind.

Early on in my adult life, pushing through feelings of fear became a defining aspect of my identity: one part personal philosophy, one part default methodology for forging the path ahead. At 23, I left my first proper job – a pretty good one! – to pursue a career of wobbly self-employment as a freelance journalist. At 24, I moved from London to Los Angeles completely alone, having only been there once before. Two years later, as my career in LA was taking off, I started a new business by myself, draining the last of my savings in the process. The year after that, I ditched my comfortable LA life to start all over again in New York. You see a theme emerging?

On the surface, this strategy worked well for me. Millennial culture encourages us to stretch ourselves to the limits of our mental and physical capabilities, especially in the quest for professional achievement. But unlike alcoholism or binge eating, workaholism is culturally sanctioned – actively encouraged, even, by a system predicated on the metrics of social influence and material wealth. My own risk-taking was rewarded with a book deal, exciting career opportunities, some flattering magazine articles. This all just served as fuel to push harder, until I felt like a spinning top with no plans of slowing down – and no idea how I could, even if I wanted to. At times, I really did. But if everything seems under control …

Life had other plans. A couple of months after I published my first book, a combination of exhaustion and injury landed me in hospital with acute back pain. It was 3 January, and a less than ideal start to the ambitious year I'd envisioned. But I found a good osteopath and quickly got back to work, albeit with a lingering sense of lethargy. By spring, I was trudging through my to-do list when a random accident put me in A&E again. This time the injury was more serious, and so was the prescription: bed rest, and a recovery time of at least three months. Suddenly, a calendar of meetings and deadlines was filled with acupuncture sessions and hospital visits. The only work to be done was to get well.

The physical pain was exacerbated by a nasty bout of impostor syndrome. As someone whose professional life is literally based on helping other people work, I felt disoriented by my unexpected incapacity to do so, even more so by my resistance to take my own advice. After years spent encouraging women to cultivate self-kindness, I was alarmed to find it almost impossible to apply such compassion to myself.

I soon learned there's no workaround for back pain. I retreated to my bed, planning to use the time to plough through a reading list I'd been too busy to tackle before. Self-improvement manuals felt like a form of masochism, so I turned to the Buddhist teachings I'd been dipping into for years, sensing that two back injuries in five months might be a sign to rethink my attitude to personal achievement. What I found was to change the way I thought about work – and fear.

Buddhism takes the prevailing ideology of western culture – that is, to approach everything from your art to your body with the mentality that you are going into battle (or about to race a really fast car) – and flips it. Rather than suggesting that you, too, can achieve greatness as long as you are willing to work harder, longer and smarter than the rest, Buddhism asks: what if you could realise how absolutely terrified you are, and … do nothing but let yourself feel it? No to-do lists. No rigorous new schedules. Just releasing the urge to out-work, out-diet, outrun your fear.

Over the course of a sweaty New York summer spent confined to my bed with my books, I underwent a period of slow realisation – less a lightbulb moment than a dimmer switch, slowly turning all the way up. Fear, I finally understood, takes many forms: some are just more socially acceptable than others. I might not be freaked out by public speaking or solo travel, but I was scared that I'd never feel successful enough; scared I'd never feel I'd worked or tried hard enough; and – more than anything – scared I would never feel like enough.

Being human is scary. It's useful to be able to face challenges with a certain amount of stoicism and grit (in fact, we probably need these emotional tools more than ever). But the real challenge is learning to view moments of insecurity as an opportunity to be terrifyingly kind to ourselves. It's not about morphing into an impenetrable super-being, but rather turning to the flawed, fragile – and yes, fearful – human being you really are, and not feeling scared of her anymore.

THE ART OF BEING ALONE

Poorna Bell

Poorna Bell is an award-winning journalist and an author, with her second book -In Search of Silence - out in May 2019. Poorna grew up believing that being alone automatically meant feeling lonely, but by pushing out of her comfort zone she has learned to enjoy her own company.

One of my earliest memories is the warmth and safety of my parents' bed.

When I was really little, I used to go into their room in the wee hours of the morning. The covers would move and I would be enveloped in blankets with their arms wrapped around me.

I know how lucky I am to have this fused into my circuitry, and it has given me an immovable sense of what love, comfort and the proximity of other people should feel like.

The idea of being alone, then, was a foreign one. I always found it easy to make friends, and at university I ran in the wolf pack that forms in that half-light of early adulthood. We lived in big groups and tiny flats, sprawled on each other's beds and floors. Even the singular experience of a break-up was cut up like pieces of cake and shared with others.

I grew up with the notion that being alone meant being lonely, and every step was taken to avoid solitude, until a time when it became necessary.

I used to be married to a man named Rob, who I loved very much. But Rob had chronic depression and he also struggled with addiction. I learned that it was possible to feel lonely even in the midst of great love and connection. Dealing with Rob's illnesses put to rest the incorrect notion of my earlier years – that being surrounded by people meant you wouldn't be touched by the long shadow cast by loneliness.

Rob's depression rendered him sometimes immobile in bed, and I realised that I was approaching a crossroads. I could either wait for him to get out of bed – and sometimes that wait seemed interminably long – or I could muster the nerve to do things on my own.

I loved my husband but I increasingly felt his illnesses were gobbling up my life, to the point where I couldn't distinguish who I was anymore outside looking after him. So I decided I had to start experiencing life again.

It started small. A lunch by myself. Going to an art gallery. I always felt the absence of him, but in the way of a phantom limb. Once I'd gained more confidence and felt less self-conscious, I went on my first holiday alone, to the Cotswolds.

It felt freeing. As a former travel journalist I had been on solo trips before, but they were always for work. Travelling alone for pleasure was filled with a different purpose. It didn't feel contingent on someone else's availability or mood. Moreover, it allowed me to think, to stretch, to expand into a vaster version of myself that wasn't micro-correcting itself because of how I thought I should behave.

Like a lot of people I'm hungry for the validation of others and being alone gave me respite from all of that, not just a break from worrying about Rob.

For a number of complicated reasons, Rob passed away in 2015 by suicide.

He died alone, far away from anyone. I hated that fact. But then I realised that even if you die surrounded by a sea of loved ones, there's something about your existence that can't be communicated to anyone else.

There was also the fact I was now, quite literally, alone. People get married for a multitude of reasons, but companionship and the sharing of a life is certainly at the top. It's such a huge commitment that recalibrating your life after it ends requires a seismic shift and effort of will.

I'm sure a lot of people pitied the fact that I was alone. But I grew to view my solitude as something that actually gave me immense strength. It meant I didn't have to wait around for people to do the things I really wanted to do. It amazes me how many women of my mother's generation don't do things that give them real pleasure, such as going on walking holidays or trips around galleries, because their spouse doesn't want to come with them. They've had to sequester a vital portion of themselves that gives them joy, because they don't feel comfortable doing it alone.

Had I waited around for other people's calendars to become free, I'd never have trekked in the Himalayas, paddleboarded down the Arno in Florence or driven along the wild west coast of New Zealand.

In some ways, I understand the discomfort. It's less about your unease in being alone, and more to do with your concern for what other people think about your solitude.

A few years ago, when Rob was alive, I took a solo trip to Dubrovnik and was dining alone in a restaurant when a couple next to me struck up a conversation. It came up that I was married, and the man said: "Oh phew, we thought it was weird you were eating alone." I bristled, but not as much as I might have done if I hadn't had a husband back home.

Nowadays, despite being minus a husband, a comment like this wouldn't make me bristle much at all. I interviewed Eric Klinenberg, professor of sociology at New York University who wrote a book called Going Solo, about the rise in the number of people living alone, and he said that when people say things like this, they're projecting their own fears. It's not you, it's them.

It's also about perspective. There's something to be said for viewing being alone as an active choice, and the incredible empowerment and strength there is to be taken from that.

It doesn't mean you don't draw comfort from being around other people, or the safety and warmth of loved ones who know you. But rather it expands your world and turns the prospect of being alone from that of a dark, bottomless chasm into a dazzlingly bright portal lit with endless possibility.

29 THINGS
I'VE LEARNED
AT 29

Emma Gannon

*Emma Gannon is the host of the popular Ctrl Alt Delete podcast
and the author of two books, the latest being The Multi-Hyphen
Method, a manual for crafting your own career. In the twilight
of her 20s, Emma reflects on what she's learned.*

Here are 29 ways I slowly but surely crept out of my comfort zone in order to feel like my 20s were worth the ups and downs, and that my 30s might be a better decade in all sorts of mysterious ways.

1. Jealousy feels icky, but it's an incredibly useful emotion. I now track what triggers me, or makes me feel vulnerable. I no longer ignore the intensity of my feelings, or swat them away like a fly. Instead I pause, sit in my uncomfortable feelings and use them as a guide. Emotions are maps.

2. Fears become more real as you get older. And that's OK. I used to be that girl who could fling a pair of knickers in a tote bag and board a flight, no problem. Now, everything seems to matter more. I have more to lose. I question everything, and therefore have grown a fear of flying. I've learned that the anxiety isn't me, but that it occasionally happens to me, and I get to decide how much of a role it plays in my life. Instead of the anxiety auditioning and getting the main part, I've made sure it only gets to play Villager Number Four who spends most of the show watching it from behind the curtain.

3. If a friend drains you, puts you down, becomes endlessly competitive with you, then it's OK to step away from them, for a while, or maybe for ever.

4. Regardless of whether or not you want to become a mother yourself one day, everything seems to melt away when you meet the newborn baby of someone close to you, no matter what other crap is going on in the world.

5. Being a feminist doesn't mean you can't ever question or call out other women for their behaviour.

6. There's more to life than work. But we do spend a lot of time at work, so let's not kid ourselves that it doesn't matter. It matters because it's your life.

7. The internet can trick you into thinking everyone's looking at you and judging you. They're not. Everyone's looking at themselves.

8. Going freelance is not a marble desk and a midday bath. It is hard, lonely and takes lots of mental health hacks and apps to keep it worthwhile.

9. Saying no will always feel difficult if (like me) you grew up being a people pleaser. But practise saying it. Saying no can becoming thrilling and addictive because it means you are reclaiming your time – and your life.

10. If you're putting something off and making up excuses not to start, it probably means you really, really want it.

11. Acknowledging your privilege is step one. Passing the mic is step two.

12. Self-sabotage is real. Any time I grow, my first inclination is to try to shrink. Monitor your reactions to your own success carefully.

13. Relationships require work and a few difficult conversations. The quicker you both say sorry, the better.

14. Digging for nuance is always more fulfilling than immediately picking a side out of peer pressure.

15. Things change. Social media platforms change. We change. Don't forget to look ahead and zoom out.

16. Journaling feels embarrassing and self-indulgent. But writing down, in pen, what you are grateful for is the best way to fall back in love with your life.

17. Any tweet you write can be taken seven billion different ways.

18. You will get bad reviews. It's OK. Search for your all-time favourite author on Amazon: even they have had a bad review.

19. It's impossible to be liked by everybody. But it can feel just as good to make something meaningful for a small number of people who really care.

20. As Caitlin Moran says: "You probably aren't having a full-on nervous breakdown – you just need a cup of tea and a biscuit."

21. Asking for more (money, effort, time) is terrifying, but ultimately thrilling. The more you ask, the more you get. Ask, ask and ask again.

22. You can do anything but you can't do everything. Keep this in mind when you are heading towards burnout.

23. In a world of content and cat videos, don't forget the art of reading. Re-reading an old book almost immediately slows me down. It's healing.

24. It's OK to contradict yourself, to be called a hypocrite, to change your mind.

25. The world is begging us to be kinder. You know when someone stands on the lefthand side of an escalator in London? People get irate. "How dare this person stand there, when I want to walk! Don't they know the rules?" But the person rarely does it because they are trying to be malicious. They simply didn't realise. Maybe they've not been to London before. We should treat people with kindness first, instead of immediately believing they are out to ruin our day.

26. Even Michelle Obama has impostor syndrome, so maybe this means it never truly goes away. Maybe it's useful to doubt ourselves, as long as it doesn't get in the way of the doing.

27. Invest in nice bedding and good shoes. "If you're not in one, you're in the other," I think the saying goes.

28. Success literally means: to achieve a desired outcome. You get to decide what the desired outcome of your life is. It can be anything. It just needs to be yours.

29. Remember you have enough inside to keep filling you up. You are your own resource. You don't need constant reassurance. You already know what you're doing. Know that you alone are totally and completely enough.

MONEY

WHY I WANT TO BE RICH

Marianne Power

Marianne Power is the author of Help Me!, a book that details a year spent living according to self-help manuals. In spite of all the advice she's absorbed, Marianne is bad with money, and has always felt ashamed of the fact that she wants to be rich. Now she wants to own it.

I have something shameful to admit: I want to be rich. There, I've said it. Do you like me less now? Do you think this makes me greedy? Grabby? A not-nice person? I've certainly thought those things in the past. I thought that being interested in money made you mean and selfish. Also, boring.

I once went to a financial coach who promised to uncover the emotional issues holding me back with my finances. After making me a cup of tea and offering me a finger of fudge, she asked me the weirdest question: "If money came to dinner, what would it be like?"

"Huh?" I replied.

She repeated the question.

"Er, I dunno, I guess he would be like a Del Boy – all brash and loud and smelling of cheap aftershave."

"Right," she replied. "And how long would you want money to stay at dinner?"

"Ten minutes, maybe?"

"So that's how long you want money to stay in your life," she replied.

That's about right, actually. Any money that hits my account flies out almost immediately. It doesn't matter how much I earn, I'll find a way to give or throw it away, often within minutes.

I've told myself it's charming and free-spirited. I've convinced myself that I'm a good person because I'm generous. I've made jokes about my expensive high-heel and hangover habit, but they're not very funny.

I'm 41 and live in a small, rented flat. I've just paid a tax bill that has almost wiped me out, and I'm bored with living this way. It's not fun to be like this – it's childish. And stupid. So why stay like this when I'm so competent in other areas of life?

It turns out our behaviour around money is not rational and is often rooted in our childhood. I learned this with the help of money expert Kate Northrup, author of Money: A Love Story. For her book Kate asked me to think of my first ever money memory and how it connects to my finances today.

The memory came instantly: I was nine, in the living room with my sister when my dad walked in. He opened his wallet and threw some notes into the air, telling us we could keep what we caught. I remember the panic, that I was going to mess up this opportunity. Fear that my sister would get more than me. Then I remember fury when my dad told me he was only joking and we had to give the money back.

To this day, I find anything to do with money stressful. I also think you don't get to keep it, so why bother holding on to it?

It's not just me. There's an idea called the Prince Charming Effect, which suggests that the reason many women don't look after their money is because they're waiting for Prince Charming to come in and sort it out. I hate the thought that I've been doing that, but maybe I have.

Have I subconsciously thought that by 'investing' in new jeans and face creams I'll look prettier and therefore be more likely to meet a man who will whisk me off into a financially secure sunset? The thought makes me cringe – which means it's probably true. But no more.

Virginia Woolf said that to write fiction a woman "must have money and a room of her own". Woolf was given the right to vote and £500 a year (from a dead aunt) at about the same time, and said the money felt infinitely more important, writing: "No force in the world can take from me my five hundred pounds." She continued: "Food, house, and clothing are mine forever. Therefore, not merely do effort and labour cease, but also hatred and bitterness. I need not hate any man; he cannot hurt me. I need not flatter any man; he has nothing to give me."

With money comes security, and with security, freedom. For women to be in their full power – for me to be in my full power – I need to sort out my cash. And that doesn't make me greedy or selfish – it's quite the opposite.

By learning about money and how to grow it, I can not only look after myself but help others, too. I can buy a home that friends and family can stay in. I can invest in companies that are doing good in the world. I can stop playing small and claim my power. It's time.

ON TOUGHENING UP

Daisy Buchanan

Daisy Buchanan is a journalist and the author of How to Be a Grown-Up and The Sisterhood. She often writes about how it's OK to feel sensitive and admit to struggle, but here she explores the idea of toughening up. In a world obsessed with self-care, how do we cultivate an inner steel?

Ever since I was a small child, I've been labouring under a misconception that has been threatening to ruin my life: the idea that suffering has a moral value. The thought that when everything goes to shit, you're scoring triple loyalty points on the Advantage Card of life, and these can eventually be cashed in for a suitable prize. You'll get into heaven. You'll meet the love of your life. You'll discover the true meaning of Christmas. It's convenient for us to believe our suffering is part of a narrative arc, that we're simply setting up the story with some end-of-first-act peril to be resolved in a final happily-ever-after. It's bleak and bewildering to discover that, as Carl Sagan said, "the universe seems neither benign nor hostile, merely indifferent". And it certainly doesn't have any plans for you.

However, this thought is also at the root of our liberation. We must take responsibility for taking care of ourselves. That might sound scary, but we've been doing it all along. If we've believed in a benign universe, it's because we've become the universe. This is where our resilience comes from. This is how we make it last.

Resilience is not a fashionable concept at the moment. It seems outdated. I was born in the mid-1980s, and for this reason alone it's widely assumed that I am incapable of toughness. Our generation has been pitched against our parents'. We march under the banner of the avocado – a fruit that is temperamental, expensive to produce, soft, easy to squash, a luxury that we have grown accustomed and entitled to. If baby boomers had an organic emblem it might be a pineapple, or a turnip – something with flesh that doesn't yield easily, which thrives in harsh conditions and gives nothing away. They tell us often that our softness is more trouble than it's worth.

If we struggle to develop resilience, I suspect it's because we were the first generation who were told failure was not an option. It's a privilege to grow up hearing you can do anything, but for many of us that privilege was tainted by the pressure of being told we had to do everything – backwards, in high heels, and get an A-star for it. As a young woman, I felt as if any failure would finish me. I was never told that not succeeding is inevitable for anyone who ever tries. It's impossible to develop resilience when you're consumed by the idea that any failure would ruin your future.

As adults, most of us fail enough to start exercising a muscle we never knew we had, to discover our strength. Resilience isn't the same as fatalism. Over time, I've made peace with my failure to get a place at Cambridge when I was 17 by telling myself my eventual university experience could not have been bettered, and if I had got in it might have been a lot less positive. That's not resilience. Resilience is being able to look myself in the eye and acknowledge I wasn't a good enough candidate. Other people's 'good' was better than my 'best' – but that doesn't make me the worst.

Resilience is acknowledging that I played a part in romances that went wrong, and that I didn't finally win a marriage by submitting myself to a series of indignities and betrayals – I learned, not just that there is no Prince Charming, but that I could be pretty charmless. I had to be better to do better. None of us are blameless. We grow up when we stop simply pointing out the craters in our personalities, hoping to be told there are no visible holes, and start the long, arduous process of filling in the gaps.

In one uncomfortable act of resilience I'll acknowledge that I can never express these ideas as well as one of my writing heroines, Joan Didion. Her essay On Self Respect is the definitive piece of work on emotional core strength. Didion wrote: "However long we postpone it, we eventually lie down alone in that notoriously uncomfortable bed, the one we make ourselves." Sometimes, this means confronting something that makes us feel very, very weak – but we might find ourselves drawing a lifetime's strength from that experience.

There's no point in suffering for its own sake, yet many of us have come to the conclusion that there might be, because we're unwittingly good at providing for ourselves when the universe falls short. We thank the fates and fear the furies when everything ultimately comes down to us.

Resilience is not, despite its assonant similarity, born of misery. It can come from early nights and early mornings, sacrifice, pleasure postponed, drinks declined. But it is defined by gain as much as pain. It's a £5 note in an old coat pocket, a chance encounter with a friend on the street and a shared, free afternoon. It's our past ghosts working to remind our future selves of our power, potential and strength.

ONIJOGBON
AND
THE VOICE

Funmi Fetto

Funmi Fetto is a contributing beauty editor at Vogue UK and the author of the forthcoming Palette: The Beauty Bible for Women of Colour. During the five years Funmi spent in Nigeria as a child, she was given the nickname Onijogbon, meaning troublesome. This sparked an exploration of how best to use her voice, even when it might make others uncomfortable.

In Dear Ijeawele: A Feminist Manifesto in Fifteen Suggestions, the Nigerian author Chimamanda Ngozi Adichie writes that she is angrier about sexism than racism. For me, however, living in England, the issue of race and racism certainly feels much more pronounced. The world I inhabit sees me as black before I'm seen as female, and so any xenophobia I experience is generally linked to the melanin in my skin. The incidents range from a woman at an art gallery party throwing her coat on me because she assumed – as I was the only person of colour in the room – I worked in the cloakroom, to a stranger on the street calling me a nigger.

And yet there is a part deep inside me that resonates with Adichie. It harkens back to the five childhood years I spent in Nigeria. There, no one was 'black'. Of course there was colourism, but sex and class were the fundamental bastions of society in which prejudice ran rife. It was and still is a culture that has an ingrained way of thinking about the roles of men and women. This school says it is scandalous and unforgivable for a woman to cheat, while it is expected and tolerated for a married man to have numerous girlfriends. (An aunt once berated me for saying I'd leave if a spouse cheated on me.)

It's still a place where a case of domestic violence where the male is the perpetrator will largely be blamed on the woman ('But why did you argue with him? I'm sure if you kept quiet, he wouldn't have beaten you'); a space where women are expected to have award-winning cookery skills ('How will you feed your husband?'); and boys are never expected to step into the kitchen. An environment where women who speak up and challenge the box into which they have been squished are seen as troublemakers. Onijogbon is a Yoruba word meaning someone who argues without giving up, someone who is stubborn in pursuing a course, or simply a troublemaker. As a young girl, it was my unofficial nickname.

When I was five, my family moved from London and for five years we lived in Lagos, the bustling cosmopolitan capital of Nigeria. I was what one would call headstrong. Even as a child, I was never the kind to back down from an argument – or a telling off. I was combative, I asked questions, I fought, I was bold, I challenged everything, I was opinionated, I used my voice often and loudly. "Onijogbon," they'd say, sometimes in frustration, sometimes anger. Sometimes in perplexity. It was used by my grandmother, aunts, uncles and my exasperated father – only in conversation with other family members because, although we understood our native tongue of Yoruba fluently, he always spoke to us in English (a remnant perhaps of colonialism and a European education). In rare moments someone would use Onijogbon as a term of endearment. For the most part it was a rebuke. And so at a young age I became aware of two things: for many, a girl using her voice is uncomfortable and unacceptable; for me, the voice was a powerful tool that could get me what I wanted but could also get me into trouble. At some point I was going to have to learn how to use it.

When I came back to London, I had the pleasure of navigating the boundaries imposed on me not only for being female but also for being black. And so I found myself using my voice to counter thoughts and opinions of westerners (male, female, young, old, middle, working and upper class), all the warped, stereotypical and erroneous concepts of Africans, immigrants, black people and black women: 'It must be terrible coming from somewhere where everyone's starving; oh, you've got your jungle dress on; you speak English surprisingly well; your hair's ugly; were you the first in your family to go to university; why do we need a black history month; did you have an arranged marriage; I'm surprised Kanye, as a black man, doesn't already have lots of illegitimate children; black people are mercenaries; you're a black woman so you must be a singer/dancer/a prostitute/ good in bed.'

Always, my speaking out – whether it was confronting mindsets or trying to have an open and honest conversation about my experiences – made people uncomfortable: I obviously had a chip on my shoulder, I couldn't take a joke, I was reading too much into it. These kind of rebukes wear you down after a while. Somewhere along the line, Onijobon became tired of making people uncomfortable, became tired of standing out and decided it was possibly easier to work on assimilating into a culture that wasn't quite adjusted to you. And so she began to stay silent.

I stayed silent for a long time. I stayed silent when I was, essentially, bullied for my faith. I stayed silent when I was leered at daily by my misogynistic male boss who later made me redundant. I stayed silent when I was refused entry into a jewellery shop because I didn't look like their regular clients, I stayed silent when I discovered I was paid significantly less than my white counterpart.

It's a fallacy that if you ignore things, they go away. Of course they don't. So, thankfully, I could only suppress my voice for so long. But something wonderful happened in my time of silence. I questioned how I used my voice. Do I need to have an opinion on everything? No. If I'm compelled to speak, do I do so even if it makes others uncomfortable? Yes. Is there a time and place for these conversations? Maybe. Is it OK to pick your battles? Sometimes ...

A new boldness came about once my voice got its second wind. Call it Onijogbon's calmer sister. My pre-quiet-time voice was driven by fury, which wasn't always productive. Now it's driven by a quiet confidence. I'm no longer self-conscious about my Christian faith. I'm unafraid to talk about money, and to ask for more of it for me and my all-female team. I will no longer make myself smaller in meetings filled with 'important white men' – or 'important white women' for that matter – just so I don't come across as intimidating, because what I have to say is no less valid. I can talk about race and female rights in the same breath as I talk about popular culture, because issues around racism and sexism should be part of the national conversation. And I don't feel pressure or the right to rail against everything I don't agree with.

Still, I have had moments where this new incarnation of my voice has failed me. Like when a stranger – a drunk man – hugged me as I walked home late one night. I felt powerless and silent. For weeks afterwards, I was enraged with myself but more so with this man who crossed my boundaries. It was a reminder that somewhere inside me Onijogbon still existed. And that was not such a bad thing.

A LETTER TO MY TIMID SELF

Farrah Storr

Farrah Storr is an author and the editor-in-chief of
Cosmopolitan. Having written The Discomfort Zone, Farrah
is all too familiar with the virtues of pushing your boundaries.
But what if she'd known this as a young girl?

Dear Me,

This is a weird one, what with me being dead and all. But I've been told I can deliver a quick message to a few key people and, well, since you're starting the life I've already lived, I thought there were a couple of things worth pointing out.

These are things I spent the longest time trying to get my head around, and now, from this vantage point, I see they make complete sense. But you don't know that yet. So see this as a sort of cheat sheet. A way of saving a lot of time and head space that could be given over to more interesting stuff, like watching blue tits eat peanuts from a cage feeder on a frosty morning. (Trust me, you'll get into this in a big way.) Don't see this as an excuse to skip the hard bits, though, because if there's one thing I can tell you as I look back now, it's that the hard bits are the ones that make all the difference …

1. You're going to hate being mixed race. You'll lie in bed at night wondering what it would be like to have blonde hair and skin the colour of a freshwater pearl. As you get older your blonde friends will tell you exactly what it's like: all that sunscreen, all that money on root touch-ups, always having to dip your head every time you walk past a building site. So instead, fantasise about the stuff that really counts, like unicorns and princes.

2. On the subject of princes, it's true, yours is not the sort of beauty that young boys will be drawn to. This will sting. At first. But on the plus side it means you won't put much store in the way you look. This is good, because beauty is a real bitch. Do not rely on it, because the only thing surer than death is that your beauty will desert you, like a shiny great helium balloon with a slow puncture. Of course, you will feel terribly sorry for yourself that, while others are out flirting at the back of Pilsworth Cinema Complex on a Saturday night, you're in bed reading a book about the life and times of Salvador Dalí. But this is what will make you beautiful in the end. Because you'll become interesting and interested in the world around you, and that's pure catnip as people get older.

3. OK, body issues. This is the one I reckon you should skip. Round about your 14th birthday you will develop a complex relationship with food. You will start to eat like a minnow – only small, thimble-size mouthfuls of dry bread a few times a day. You will hate your muscular legs. You will wish damnation on your round, cantilevered bottom and teeny tiny waist. Your periods will eventually depart. Your hair, your lovely, glossy hair will turn to ash. And day by day you will start to fade. Instead, spend your youth eating! In particular Macintosh's Mint Toffos which they'll inexplicably discontinue a few years later (sacrilege!) And remember, people tend not to look at the size of your hips or the shape of your thighs, only the size and shape of your smile. So make it as big and toothy as you can. Every single day.

4. Oh, and you won't get into Oxford University. Sorry about that. You will think this is a great big diversion on your path to becoming 'somebody' but the truth is the Saturday job you take cleaning glasses at Granada Studio Tours is far more vital in shaping who you go on to become. So savour every minute.

5. And yes, you're going to fall in love with a few highly unsuitable men. Go ahead, do it. It's important to know what a bad relationship looks like, so when you're in a good one that hits a few bumps you know the difference.

6. Basically, life will feel like a grind a lot of the time. And this is exactly how it should feel. Don't shirk from challenge, but seek it out. Know that obstacles are put in front of you, not to trip you up, but to reveal what you're really made of. And if you get through life and you've never failed then you've never really pushed yourself.

Know all this and you will have a brilliant, challenging and rewarding life. Good luck. I'll be watching.

Farrah x

Alice-Azania Jarvis
Lindsey Hilsum
Mina Holland
Natasha Lunn
Pandora Sykes
Gillian Orr
Nellie Eden
Anna Jones

RELATIONSHIPS

CONVERSATIONS WITH MY MOTHER

Alice-Azania Jarvis

Alice-Azania Jarvis is a journalist and founder of The Sunday Salon podcast and events series. Her mother grew up in a psychiatric hospital and became an actress in cult horror films. They sit down for a mother-daughter chat about their very different life experiences.

There are things I've always known about my mother. She grew up in a psychiatric hospital where my grandfather was a doctor in the 1940s and 1950s. She was a famous actress in the 1970s thanks to roles in Hammer Horror films and in the soap Crossroads. And she gave all that up when she had me. What I didn't know until recently is that her mother was an alcoholic who had profound depression. And that she had been sexually assaulted in her 20s. These facts, along with many others, came spilling out one afternoon as we sat on my parents' bed, a Dictaphone between us.

I'd decided to use the Christmas break to interview her. I'm 34 and my mother, Judy Matheson, is 73. I feel ashamed of how one-way our relationship is. Despite the obviously interesting nature of what I did know, I'd never asked more. And I call myself a journalist! How many of us ever stop to think of the women our mothers are? The people they were before we arrived – and still are, entirely independent of us?

As my mother and I sat there, we were fleetingly reduced to almost-strangers, fumbling over uncharted, sometimes uncomfortable, conversational rocks. But it was also exhilarating, an experience I'd recommend to anyone.

Afterwards, I was struck by how the conversation began small – personal details, family minutiae – but became big, encompassing life in postwar Britain, women in the workplace, reproductive rights, mental health. We devour period dramas and history books – and yet we often overlook the richest resources right in front of us.

—

AAJ: I want to start by talking about our generations, because you often see yours, baby boomers, pitted against mine, millennials. The conventional wisdom is that you had it easy, whereas we graduated into a recession.

JM: It's never helpful to pit people against one another! Though I wouldn't say my generation had it easy, particularly women. Things were much less convenient. My mother did all the family laundry by hand. There was great inequality in terms of education: if you passed the 11-plus you went to a grammar school, which was academic, but if you didn't you went to a secondary modern. It was very divisive. And of course we never went abroad.

AAJ: You were born in August 1945, as the Second World War was ending. What was that like?

JM: It was just how you lived. I remember going to a sweet shop in the village, South Ockendon in Essex, and counting out my rations. And we didn't have central heating – just a two-bar electric fire in the sitting room.

AAJ: You had quite an unusual childhood, in that you grew up in a psychiatric hospital …

JM: South Ockendon Hospital. My father was the head doctor and we lived in a big house on the grounds. The patients would come for tea and there was a recreation hall where you could put on plays and have dances.

AAJ: And your mother struggled with her mental health?

JM: I didn't know that until I was older, but I knew she was an alcoholic, which caused me huge angst. I'd worry about bringing home school friends, and became very sensitive to even the slightest slurring. On the other hand, I remember lovely things like her taking me for baked beans on toast in a cafe. It's quite difficult to reconcile these images. It was thought she was suffering manic depression, but it was just sort of ignored. Depression wasn't spoken about the way it is today. She was on very strong medication. Much later on, she suffered delusions and tried to kill herself, and went to the psychiatrist William Sargant at St Thomas's in London for electroconvulsive therapy. I think she was very unsatisfied with her life. She'd been a nurse before – and this was a typical case of a highly intelligent woman not being able to express herself in work or anything creative. In those days, even in the 1960s, careers were not really something to be aspired to as women.

AAJ: You went to the New College of Speech and Drama in Hampstead. It must have been amazing to be in London in the 1960s.

JM: Yes, in the 1950s we'd all been dressing like old ladies and going to hops – then it all changed. I can remember hearing The Beatles for the first time at a party in Brentwood in 1962, and I was very aware of the new hairstyles, the clothes and Biba. At the weekends we'd go out clubbing to the Cafe des Artistes in Chelsea where The Rolling Stones used to play, as well as the Flamingo Club on Wardour Street.

AAJ: Was everyone having sex outside marriage?

JM: I think so. The sexual revolution was ahead of itself, because everybody says the pill freed women, but it wasn't readily available. Contraception was a kind of undercover thing – you talked about it privately and went to Marie Stopes off Goodge Street to get fitted for a diaphragm. Most other clinics wouldn't countenance taking unmarried women, which is why we muttered to each other: "Go to Marie Stopes." There were a lot of backstreet abortions, too. Vera Drake, Mike Leigh's film, was very familiar to us all.

AAJ: There's been an explosion of debate about sexual boundaries with the #MeToo movement. What was your experience? You did quite sexy films: Hammer Horrors, Confessions of a Window Cleaner. Did you feel objectified?

JM: Personally, I didn't. I embraced second-wave feminism and I was pretty voluble with it. I never saw playing sexy roles as being at odds with that. That said, nudity was expected, and I was never totally comfortable. I was always grateful for the wardrobe mistress standing by with a dressing gown.

I'm completely supportive of #MeToo. There were a lot of things my generation put up with because they weren't discussed which in retrospect were totally unacceptable. I often look back on one particular experience I had with another actor, older and quite well-known, who I'd have dinner with sometimes, entirely platonically – we had a long-standing platonic friendship. One evening I went back to his flat for coffee and he leapt on me. I didn't know what to do, so I went along with it but afterwards I ran home, more angry than upset.

AAJ: You were married twice but you had children late – you were 39 when you had me and 45 when you had my sister. Why did you give up your career?

JM: I didn't think I'd given up. I thought I'd just throw you in the back of the car and go off to work – but it was bloody hard work, so staying at home just materialised. Did I feel unfulfilled? No – perhaps if I'd been younger that might have been different.

AAJ: Now you're in your 70s you've had a career renaissance – there are fan tributes on YouTube, and you appear at a lot of horror conventions. How did that happen?

JM: It's so strange. You get an IMDb page. Then Wikipedia appeared, and the tributes. Somebody else started up a Facebook page. Then five years ago, I was approached about doing conventions. At first I was like: "No way." I was frightened because I hadn't done anything for years and I looked so different. But they don't expect you to look the same. Now I've been all over the country.

AAJ: Looking back over your life, what are biggest changes you've seen happen?

JM: Life has been transformed by mobile phones. When each of my parents died I was informed by public phone. When I was growing up there were no real supermarkets and no frozen food. Public transport has got 100% better. And I'd never been on a plane until I was 21 and went on a theatre tour to America.

AAJ: Something we are examining as a society at the moment is our attitude towards ageing – and towards older women. What has your experience been?

JM: I did go through a mini confidence crisis around 50. I was very confused about what clothes to wear – I'd always worn things like leopard print but I wasn't sure if it was still appropriate. We know now it is, of course! And there comes a time when you feel less visible which can be hard – but not really, in the great pantheon of hardships.

Then there are the good things: I care a lot less what people think now. I've loved the internet: it's given me a whole new lease. I love social media – it makes me laugh, gives me my information. I've never had what you call "haters".

And the thing about ageing, really, is that it's so much better than the alternative, isn't it? So that's my philosophy.

DEAR
MARIE

Lindsey Hilsum

*Lindsey Hilsum is the international editor of Channel 4 News
and author of In Extremis, a biography of war correspondent
Marie Colvin, a friend and colleague of Lindsey's who died
covering the siege of Homs in Syria. Lindsey spent seven years
researching Marie's life. Here she writes a letter saying goodbye.*

Dear Marie,

This is weird, isn't it? I've learned more about you since
you were killed than in all the years we knew each other.
If you'd survived that rocket attack in Syria, I would never
have written your biography. I wouldn't have walked in your
footsteps from Oyster Bay high school to the beach, as you
used to do when you were 16, when you went to have a spliff
with Tommy and the other kids. I met Tommy, by the way.
Sweet guy! But you never stuck with the sweet guys, did you?
He put me onto Chris who was more your type: dangerous, a
bit out of control, from the wrong side of the tracks. Chris is
building boats in Maine now. Came off the drugs and drink
when he was 28, and lives a healthy life by the sea. He had
great stories of how you and he used to sneak out at night
and break into people's gardens to go skinny-dipping in their
pools. He said he went to your funeral and your mum was
really nice to him.

Your teenage diaries were very funny and almost made me
regret having destroyed my own (I shredded them 20 years
ago). My favourite part is when you were 13 and started
to defy your parents, insisting on wearing shorts to school
and going out with boys. And the weekly arguments about
going to Mass. I loved that entry: "To church. Wore mini.
The mother and the father no like." It made me laugh out
loud. But you never neglected your schoolwork – you were
always top of the class. I think that's what made you a great
journalist: the combination of rebellion and diligence. I really
enjoyed researching your early years, but a couple of our

male colleagues – no prizes for guessing who – wrote reviews of the biography saying the section on your childhood and adolescence was boring. They cheered up hugely when I got to all the wars you covered. I wanted to call and tell you because I knew you would have laughed at how predictable they are!

Quite often, mid-writing, I wanted to call you to sort out some conundrum or other, because there were occasions when what you wrote in the diaries and what others remembered didn't chime. I could imagine you laughing and saying: 'Come over, let's have a drink and I'll tell you what really happened.' I caught you out a couple of times, though. You were a bit of a fibber, weren't you? Not in your journalism – which was pure – nor in the diaries. But in what you told others about yourself. That story about overhearing your first husband's lover talking about him on the bus from Baghdad to Amman in 1991 – it took me ages to find out that it wasn't true because she was never in Baghdad. But half a dozen people told me that you had told them the story. I guess it heightened the drama, and boy, did you love a bit of drama. By the tenth retelling I bet you believed it.

It's a rule that we journalists are not supposed to make ourselves the story, but I broke that one. How does it feel to have been made into a legend? It's not just the book of course, but the film. I'm pretty sure you'd like being played by Rosamund Pike – I think she really 'got' you. And she's super glamorous, of course, and who wouldn't want a beautiful film star to play them? It's interesting how many young women tell me they like the book. On one hand, it's good they relate to someone adventurous and independent like you, but on the other I wouldn't want them to be so careless with themselves. It's not just that you went in further and stayed longer in warzones than the rest of us, but the way you conducted your personal life. If any guy had a neon sign on his head saying 'date briefly but do not marry' you went right in there. And, Marie, you suffered so much after you were injured and lost the sight in your eye. I never realised what a front you were putting on when inside you were falling apart. I wish I'd understood that when you were alive.

I loved those lists of songs and lyrics in your diaries. Thank you for introducing me to Lucinda Williams and getting me to listen to more Emmylou Harris and Bonnie Raitt. You loved a country song full of faithless men and broken women. I would listen to them when writing. I felt your physical presence very strongly. Everyone has their rituals for not writing (another cup of coffee, tidying the sock drawer). Mine is online shopping. It's amazing I didn't bankrupt myself with the hours spent perusing clothes websites rather than getting down to work. I bought this soft mole-grey leather jacket, thinking, I've never had a leather jacket before, but now is the moment. When it arrived, I put it on and realised that it was exactly the kind of jacket you would wear. I'd kind of morphed into you.

I keep thinking of February 2012 when you were killed in Baba Amr. You'd already given the lie to Syrian government propaganda that everyone in the besieged suburb was a terrorist, by reporting on the "widows' basement" where the women and children were sheltering. You were out and safe. But you went back. I couldn't understand why. I still don't.

You felt you were abandoning the people because you could leave and they couldn't. But in the end you abandoned us – your family, your friends, the other journalists covering Syria, the readers who only knew what was happening because of your reporting. I understand that you were committed to telling the story but I think you had grown reckless with your own safety. Why didn't you call me before you went back? Well, I know the answer to that – you didn't want to hear me tell you not to do it. So, by the time you called it was too late. I will never forget that last conversation by Skype. I woke up the next morning to hear the news of your death and realised that I would never speak to you again.

I've finished writing your book, and it's out there. I hope you like it. I certainly didn't hold back on your flaws, I didn't portray you as St Marie. But you wouldn't have wanted that, would you? You've been dead seven years – that's the length of time most religions decree for mourning, isn't it? So I think we finally have to part. That's not going to be easy for me, after all this time we've spent together. I've got to know you so well, and yet I still have so many questions. I suppose they'll have to remain unanswered.

Goodbye, Marie. I'm going to miss you.

Love,

Lindsey xx

ON MY PARENTS

Mina Holland

Mina Holland is an editor at The Guardian and the author of two books on food. Although the title of her second work is Mamma, she has rarely written about family. Here, she considers the trials and tribulations of parenting as she prepares to welcome her first child.

"Friends are God's apology for relations" is a favourite saying of my dad's, one of a few he likes to throw into conversation with the family over early evening gin and nuts. Being casually insulted in this way feels a part of my DNA, the quote now so familiar it's taken on a kind of cosiness – Dad's counterpart, somehow, to Mum's banana bread, both confirming I'm back in the family home.

In fact, so familiar is it that I was surprised to discover recently it's not a line of Dad's, but of the sardonic late British journalist Hugh Kingsmill. Despite being written in the first half of the 20th century, Kingsmill's words strike me as open to contemporary – millennial, even – interpretation. The idea that our friends can be the family we choose is the kind of empowering sentiment advocated by the self-help industry. There's a feminist message in there, too, encouraging us modern women to forge a future away from the domestic sphere and the relationships into which we were born.

While on one level I like this idea of my friendship group as a self-curated family – each friend answering a need within me, and I within them, to make for a complete line-up of emotionally rewarding relationships – I've never thought it capable of replacing my actual relations. Not that I'd want it to. I'm lucky enough to have a stable family unit within which there's no shortage of love and support, but also no deficit in the kind of dysfunction the west deems needing of therapeutic attention. I love my parents, but they drive me mad.

I've long held the belief that the hardest thing about coming of age – harder than heartbreak, debt and the loss of blissful ignorance – is accepting your parents' fallibility. Or, better

put, in becoming comfortable with questioning the outlook
you inherit from them. Until your teens, the notion that your
mum and dad are right forms the delicate crumb of what is
certain and true and right, before its edges start to crispen
and perhaps crumble away (excuse the cake metaphor: I'm a
food writer – it's what I know, and I'm hungry). You spend
your early life looking for guidance from these people who
are really no more than someone else's children themselves,
questioning the sureties and rules with which they were
raised (and which were probably more rigid than yours). For
me, navigating my parents' views and behaviours has been a
20-year process of setting them – and my childhood – into
sharp relief. I've acquired experience, met people, made
relationships, found new contexts and learned to do things
my own way, all of which may not, and often do not, chime
with their ways.

On the eve of motherhood – my daughter is due on
International Women's Day – I'm questioning what I want to
take forward and what I want to leave behind. Maybe what is
both most wonderful and terrifying about family is belonging
– the comfort and the horror of where we're from and its
unchangeability.

I feel at once defined by and contemptuous of my parents'
eccentricities: their low regard for fashion or even good taste
(think a beautiful Victorian cabinet on a zebra print rug,
the insistence that their fake Christmas tree is lovely); their
admirable thriftiness; the way they communicate in code
(or not at all); their tendency to give everyone a nickname
– even their unborn granddaughter, who they're calling

Pagan because we're not sure we'll christen her. I feel inspired and frustrated by my mother's unwavering kindness, her determination to see the good in even the greatest of arseholes, her gentle but confusing way with words, and also tickled and annoyed by her proclivity for non-sequiturs, refusal to learn to use Google Maps or to correctly pronounce Ottolenghi. I feel kinship with my dad's taking of strong positions and his hot temper, in awe of his quick wit and intellect, and also maddened by his view that buying good quality meat is a luxury, not a responsibility. Just when I think I could combust with resolutions not to inflict their ways on my about-to-be daughter, I remember I wouldn't want them to be anyone else, and that – forgive the schmaltz – all this is part of me.

I realise much of this comes from a place of privilege, of having a family in the first place, one I love and (in some ways, more importantly) that I like – most of the time. We've had our share of blazing rows, betrayals and dependencies, but I know my good fortune in having them. Whatever your family circumstances – whether or not you know them, like them or speak to them – we are all from somewhere, and it's my belief that we need to let this inform but not define us.

On this, the American writer and activist Audre Lorde speaks to me: "The strongest lesson I can teach my son is the same lesson I teach my daughter: how to be who he wishes to be for himself. And the best way I can do this is to be who I am and hope that he will learn from this not how to be me, which is not possible, but how to be himself." There are lessons here for readers not just about how to parent, but how to negotiate our parental and subsequent influences: that we must find our own voice amid the din of family, which might sometimes compete with how we experience the world; that having children is about making individuals, not propagating our own values; that knowing our position on everything from the Big Questions to how to roast potatoes – and to how we relate to others – will help give our children the tools to do this for themselves.

So, in response to Hugh Kingsmill, I would say that though my friends are great, God doesn't need to apologise for my relations. He could, however, say sorry for my parents' zebra print rug. And let's hope that, in 2019, they'll have a real Christmas tree with which to welcome their Pagan granddaughter.

THE
DISCOMFORT
OF INTIMACY

Natasha Lunn

Natasha Lunn is the features editor at Red magazine and founder of the Conversations on Love newsletter. In her 20s, she believed being single was outside her comfort zone. When she entered into a relationship, however, she realised it was intimacy she found difficult, because it requires vulnerability, courage and a leap of faith.

We all tell and believe stories about who we are. Sometimes, those stories begin with the way our friends or families react to us as we grow up. Other times, we make them up to protect ourselves from complicated insecurities. The unhelpful upshot is that after we've told or believed a certain story for too many years, it can start to feel like the truth.

In my 20s the story I believed about myself was this: I was a person trying – and failing – to find intimacy. In the love stories of my life I had written myself as the victim, a woman who was difficult to love, who asked for too much and yet too little, and who couldn't make a relationship last. The truth, however, was that as much as I craved intimacy, I was resisting it.

I was self-absorbed and immature. I thought being in a long-term relationship would be well within my comfort zone, as satisfying as pushing the final piece of a jigsaw into place. What I hadn't considered is that real intimacy is one of the most complicated things we can do as humans because it forces us to look honestly at our values, imperfections, childhoods and identities. It demands that we stop hiding from ourselves and from others. It requires us to confront our flaws, then find the courage to show them to another person and ask them to love us in spite of them. (And, just as hard, to do the same for them.)

It's easy to underestimate the challenges of intimacy because, in stories, it's rarely described as the continuously unfolding experience that it is. I'd argue that's why some of us are underprepared for sharing a life with another person.

There's a James Baldwin quote on intimacy I think about often. He wrote: "Love takes off masks that we fear we cannot live without and know we cannot live within." For a decade I wore masks in relationships: I curated 'cool' Spotify playlists for boyfriends rather than songs I was actually listening to; I wore makeup to bed, afraid a boyfriend would see my pores, and then felt ashamed when my foundation left a stain on the pillow. If I felt insecure in the early stages of a relationship or sensed someone slipping away, I'd retreat and pretend to be busy for two weeks, rather than sensibly asking: "What's really going on here?" (Faking aloofness never works, for the record.)

The way I resisted intimacy was by never really showing my whole self to anybody. Since I saw myself as the unlovable victim, I wasn't taking responsibility for being dishonest about who I really was. I also hadn't pulled back from my fantasies of the men I dated to see them for who they really were.

And then, love forced me to take off my mask. I met a primary school teacher who was good at keeping plants alive and making me laugh. He was clever and kind and remarkable. I wish I could tell you I had matured enough to find the courage to be myself. The reality is that after six months of dancing around the edges of intimacy, I ate a dodgy salami baguette at the airport and spent 24 hours vomiting out of my mouth and nose in front of him. He made a camp bed outside the loo and held my clammy hand throughout the night. The experience snapped my 'cool girl' protective shield in two. It was humbling and it was gross; it was the start of something honest.

Meeting the man who would become my husband wasn't a pushing-the-final-piece-of-a-jigsaw-into-place moment, more a slow and clumsy lesson in self-awareness. Because, aged 30, although I'd been in love before, I'd never experienced true intimacy.

What I've learnt on this sometimes uncomfortable, always interesting journey is that there will probably be some discomfort from your childhood or past relationships that bubbles up again as you fall in love. It might be that your parent was unreliable, so when your partner doesn't stick to a plan it makes you anxious. Or that they were emotionally unavailable, which means you're particularly sensitive if a partner seems distant. As well as better understanding our own reactions, paying attention to the subtext of feelings can help us see that if we're annoying a partner it might not even be about us at all – maybe our behaviour has reminded them of an experience from their past. Knowing this stopped me from seeing every niggle or argument as a sign of either my or my husband's flaws, more just a natural part of living a life with another person.

One of the hardest parts of intimacy is that, when you argue, the stakes are higher. I have learnt that saying fears out loud ('I feel jealous about X' or 'it hurt me when you did Y') can make a problem smaller. And that walking back from an argument is about practice; the trick is to catch yourself before you say the thing you know will hurt them the most. After my husband and I had a fight last year – which was, I'll admit, mostly my fault – I stomped upstairs to brush my teeth in a rage. A few minutes later, he came into the bathroom, handed me a glass of water and said: "I'm still angry at you. I still love you." Intimacy is understanding that both things can be true in one moment. And next time, it will be my turn to sidestep my pride and offer a truce disguised as a glass of water.

It took me years to see the discomfort of intimacy as one of the most valuable experiences of my life. Perhaps if we had more stories of real long-term love, I'd have recognised this sooner, and if I'd had more practice at dropping my masks, I'd have learned to love myself sooner, too. But there are no shortcuts to intimacy and sometimes you have to learn by getting it wrong – by saying the hurtful thing and then regretting it, by acting jealous and then understanding why, by snapping over a partner's mistake before realising you make plenty yourself. It turns out that when you forgive yourself for your own flaws, it's much easier to forgive someone else's.

Today I'm still a novice in intimacy, but now I realise I no longer have to run away from my vulnerabilities. They are, after all, what make us a whole person, and you can't hold back parts of yourself if you really want to love and be loved. I know showing someone your whole, imperfect, beautiful heart is hard. I also know it's worth it.

BOOKS FOR MY DAUGHTER

Pandora Sykes

Pandora Sykes is a journalist and the co-host of weekly current affairs and pop culture podcast The High Low. Her Instagram account is awash with reading recommendations – from the latest New Yorker profile to Man Booker nominated novels. Here she looks at books through a more personal lens, compiling a list of titles filled with lessons to pass on to her daughter, Zadie.

Reading is my salvation, something that both energises and calms me. Working your way through a book can be the best therapy and – if you curate your shelves wisely – the ultimate education. I've learned about life's weightier subjects – such as sex, equality, the meaning of true love – through reading. And I hope my baby daughter does, too. Here are a few books that have helped me navigate some of the toughest lessons. Now I'm passing them on to Zadie to learn from as she grows up. I hope she falls in love with them all.

Goodnight Mr Tom *by Michelle Magorian*

I read this when I was nine, and it was my first experience of a really sad story. I gulped it down in one afternoon (I was a voracious reader, even as a little girl), curled up in a ball on my bed. Goodnight Mr Tom taught me about my own privilege: here was a boy my age, who had been emotionally deprived, while I was wrapped in love. When my mother asked me if I was enjoying it, I blinked back furious tears – the injustice of it all! – and pulled her into a hug. It's a beautiful, heart-wrenching book about how family doesn't always come in conventional forms. I'll give it to Zadie to read when she's nine years old, so that she may realise that happiness is not a gift given to every child – just the very lucky ones.

The Course of Love *by Alain de Botton*

I love modern philosophy – Milan Kundera's The Unbearable Lightness of Being turned my world upside down when I read it aged 17 – and nobody beats Alain de Botton on romance. I grew up believing romantic love was a fairy tale; that I had to kiss a lot of frogs before my prince rescued me (and Christ, did I kiss some frogs). The Course of Love taught me that love is a process of negotiation and compromise, not of sacrifice. I dip into this book time and time again for its diplomacy and rationality, and I hope it will offer the same salve to Zadie in her future romances.

Matilda *by Roald Dahl*

If you were to ask which author has made the biggest impact on my life, then the answer would probably be Roald Dahl. And not just for his children's books – Matilda, The Twits, The Witches – but also for his autobiography, Boy, and frankly creepy short stories such as those in Kiss Kiss. I've chosen Matilda because it really conveys the magic of reading. And I think reading is magic, even if you lack the protagonist's awesome spellworking abilities.

We Should All Be Feminists

by Chimamanda Ngozi Adichie

To be honest it's hard to recommend just one book by Adichie because I'd like my daughter to read all of them. But this slender tome already resides on Zadie's bookshelf, a birth gift from my friend Teresa – nestled in between Chimp and Zee and When I Am Big – which makes it a good place to start. I hope the cultural topography of western society will be very different by the time Zadie's a teenager, and that this book will read as a relic of a time when women had to fight to be heard. In truth, I expect we'll have made only baby steps in that time. In which case this book will be as relevant as ever to the young woman in my charge.

One Day by David Nicholls

This book completely undid me. In fact, it undoes me – because I re-read it on average once a year. I think people who don't like One Day are missing a piece of their heart, quite frankly. I don't see this as a traditional love story, but rather a testament to the endurance of friendship (which is arguably a much better narrative than any tale about sex). So many writers I know were and are inspired by this book; it's a deep study of the psychology of people which reveals that, sometimes, even the best of us act like utter dickheads. Not a bad lesson for Zadie to learn, that.

Polo by Jilly Cooper

There are many books to turn to when it comes to learning about sex. Judy Blume's Forever is a popular choice (although Ralph freaked me out a bit) but my sex education came almost entirely from Jilly Cooper. I probably shouldn't have been reading her books aged 11 (I pilfered them from my two older sisters) but they gave me such a healthy understanding of sex (even if, in a pre-Google world, I didn't understand what all the words meant). The women in Cooper's novels are full-bushed and pleasure-driven, rather than passive objects. While there will be inevitably far more woke (and, er, appropriate) books for Zadie to learn about sex, I'll definitely encourage her to devour a few of Cooper's bonkbusters, even just to put a smile on her face.

Fight Like a Girl *by Clementine Ford*

This is a furious sizzler of a book and it fired me up more than anything I've ever read. I learned so much from it about the galvanising force of anger and how it can help others. I went to an all-girls school from the age of four to 18 and, as a result, I saw boys and men as other. I fetishised them and their every quotidian act (watching a boy pick up a highlighter in the Leeds University library, aged 19, I'd think: they highlight just like us!). I moulded parts of myself to try to win the attention of someone I liked. The only man I've never done that for is now my husband. I'd like Zadie to read it as a teenager, so she interacts with men (whether romantically or platonically) from a place of strength.

White Teeth *by Zadie Smith*

People ask me all the time if my husband and I named our baby after Zadie Smith. We didn't – like my own name, Zadie is from Greek mythology – but we're tickled by the association. Not only is Smith one of my favourite authors, but my daughter will also grow up in NW10, the postcode in which the author set so many of her books. I'd love Zadie to dive into the literary past of her neighbourhood, told through such a diverse and assured cast of characters. White Teeth, Smith's first novel, is one of the writer's best.

ON TURNING INTO YOUR MOTHER

Gillian Orr

*Are all women destined to turn into their mums one day?
The content director at Refinery29, Gillian Orr, whose mother
firmly believes the answer is yes, questions the inevitability of
the sentiment.*

My mother has many beliefs. One drink is too many, two is never enough – that's one. Never cancel a holiday to attend a funeral is another. But her most sacred mantra is that a woman will inevitably turn into her mother. Try as you might, her spectre will hunt you down and, before you know it, you're announcing to a crowd: "One drink is too many …" Yeah, you've got the picture.

The dating advice she gave my brothers was that if they wanted to know what a girlfriend would be like when she was older, they should look at her mother. The girlfriend would slowly morph into Mrs Whoever, making the same meatball spaghetti and telling the same jokes. And having been happily married for 40 years, it was my mother's logic that I should seek out someone like my father. Thanks, Mum, I'll send you my therapist's bill.

She has a point, though. My mother and grandmother both grew up in Australia, while I was raised in the UK. Gran passed away a few years back, but our (mostly) telephone relationship means I have a firm memory of her voice. As my own mum gets older, I sometimes think I've dialled into the afterlife when I call home for our Monday night chat. It's the same intonation as Gran; the same laugh; same… nagging. It's all familiar to me: the way she goes into excruciating detail about a trip to Sainsbury's; that she'll always bring the peanuts from the plane home with her; that she has taken up bridge.

It's quite frightening, really. But the transformation took a while – Mum was in her 60s before I noticed it. I know a few women in their 30s who are already transitioning. Someone I went to university with actually wears Phase Eight.

So where does that leave me? Should I start putting henna in my hair and smoking Silk Cut now? This would be ambitious when I'm blonde and, quite frankly, no one cool ever smoked a Silk Cut. And, by the way, if you need a further excuse to throw away those cigarettes, a 2009 report by the American Society of Plastic Surgeons found that women's faces tended to follow their mothers' in terms of sagging. Cool.

There have been studies into how women conduct themselves as they age. Contemporary neuroscience indicates that our mothers, traditionally the primary caregivers, programme our behaviour from an early age, by sheer presence. We then change as we interact with others and create new patterns in our brain. But, just when you thought you were out of the woods, our neurons seek familiar paths, particularly in stressful situations. That's why you suddenly sound like Mummy Dearest when you have road rage.

"All women become like their mothers. That is their tragedy. No man does, and that is his," said Oscar Wilde. So maybe it's not all bad. But what if you want to make your own path? The customary narrative is that men are supposed to live up to their father, women to not be like their mother. It makes sense that in the past women followed in their mother's footsteps – they didn't have a lot of choice. But with more paths and power available to us now, perhaps things will change.

I'm already starting to see some similarities with my own mother. Put it this way: the grape doesn't fall far from the vine. So perhaps my fate awaits me. But for now, at least, I revel in our differences – and I do think you should always go to that funeral.

TYPICAL
GIRLS

Nellie Eden

Nellie Eden is the associate editor of Dazed Beauty, co-founder of the creative agency Babyface, and a freelance journalist. While she's always felt drawn to the don't-give-a-damn attitude of punk musicians, it's not something she's been able to cultivate for herself. In this essay, she unpacks the notion of likability.

Don't create
Don't rebel
Have intuition
Can't decide

Typical girls get upset too quickly
Typical girls can't control themselves
Typical girls are so confusing
Typical girls – you can always tell
Typical girls don't think too clearly
Typical girls are unpredictable (predictable)

I'm watching a grainy video on YouTube of 25-year-old
Viv Albertine, 14-year-old Ari Up and 24-year-old Palmolive
throwing themselves around a bandstand in a nondescript
English park. This is the video for The Slits' first single,
Typical Girls, released in 1979. I am nodding my head 'yes',
trying to catch the slightest hint of a rhythm. There is none.

In all honesty it sounds pretty terrible, and that's why I
absolutely love it. It's so unapologetic. The Slits are the kind of
girls who'd drag you to the best house party you've ever been
to, then beat you up and shag your boyfriend. Po-faced feral
roughnecks earnestly screeching ironic political statements at
nobody in particular, while dressed as Neverland's lost boys
and kicking the air about them. This is why I worship female
punk musicians. They just don't give a damn, do they?

I can't say the same for myself. I spend a lot of time really
wanting people to like me. Not everyone, not all the time,
but most of the time – and it bores me to death. I think
it's a feeling many women will be able to identify with. I've

left meetings hoping I smiled enough, walked out of dates obsessed by whether I made a good impression. When leaving dinner parties and worrying the whole bus ride home if I'd asked enough good questions, I'd also invariably be feeling the most in love with the more cantankerous or moody guests I'd shared the night with. Which begs the question: if my idols decidedly don't care about being liked, why has the desire to be affable dogged me since day dot?

The answer is gendered. I am, as a female, contextualised as the object. My success as a person is deeply enmeshed with how people receive me. I must be digestible. I've known this to be true as much as I know my own name. I've been told about dangerous women who operate on the fringes of society and how vulnerable that's made them.

I raise my voice an octave on the phone so salespeople might think of me as polite. When I found my Uber rating was lower than a bunch of my friends', I carried guilt around with me for days. I've used plainer English on dates so guys don't feel spoken down to, and I've grinned until my teeth hurt during job interviews. Often, at night, when I'm in bed next to my boyfriend, I'll ask him questions to find out how others perceive me. I always wrap them up as something else, but he sniffs me out. I know this isn't my fault, this need to be liked, but I always feel disappointed when he asks, through the dark in a whisper: 'Why do you care, Nell?'

As women, we have been raised to ingratiate ourselves. Thanks to thousands of years of social conditioning, we've been trained as peacekeepers, negotiators, hosts and mediators, roles that could also read as nice, well behaved, desirable. I'm aware it's a sweeping statement, and more power to you if it doesn't apply. But there's no doubt that the currency of popularity has never been as visible as it is today. Being liked has officially surpassed being brilliant or different.

And why is that? Social media. The bland positivity, the empty grins and the lively captions of apps like Instagram send me into a gloomy inertia. Who could have predicted the impact an app would have on a generation of people? Now, 'liked' or 'like' have a different meaning from 10 years ago, having less to do with conversation, charisma or real interactions. I feel strongly, like lots of my peers, that today's societal pressures are about presenting an idealised version of yourself that's palatable to a broad spectrum of people.

I don't think the pressures are the same for men. My male peers are rewarded for their brusqueness at work while I've received criticism for being 'forthright' in meetings. My twin brother categorically doesn't feel the need to leave everyone in the room feeling warm and fuzzy about themselves.

For me, music has been a way out of performing niceness. My favourite frontwomen definitely don't lie awake worrying about what people think of them. I also know what I think about people who try to be liked. I think bending to the will of others blunts one's independent thought, smothers personality and quashes the ability to act out of desire. It renders you mass, mainstream, pliant. It makes you typical.

What a good angsty upbringing and interest in subculture do allow for is a plethora of antiheroes to look up to. My heroes are women who embody Viv's anti-conformism. Punks, in the traditional sense: Kim Gordon, Neneh Cherry and Poly Styrene, but also Dolly Parton, Chimamanda Ngozi Adichie, Meadow in The Sopranos and Alexandria Ocasio-Cortez. Great women who have changed things don't all look the same. I don't think you have to tie socks in your hair or pin badges to a leather jacket to be punk. I think anyone who asks questions and does things differently ought to be applauded – especially if they happen to be female.

When I listen to The Slits, I remember myself. I'm slowly forcing my learned social behaviours to change. I say sorry a lot less, but old habits die hard.

I'd rather be searching out the truth than have an invitation to a party every Friday night. As my favourite, Viv, puts it: "I have burned all my bridges for the sake of getting as near as I can to the truth. And after years of searching for the truth, you find that that's all you can bear. The truth and nothing but the truth."

Fingers crossed, I'll be an unpleasant woman soon.

ON
MOTHERHOOD

Anna Jones

Anna Jones is a chef, stylist and writer specialising in vegetarian food. Her cookbooks, among them the award-winning Modern Cook's Year, include a number of child-friendly recipes which nod to her three-year-old son, Dylan. Like many women, Anna has found motherhood joyous but also difficult. Here she opens up about her journey.

Motherhood. I'm three years in, and I still haven't even begun to work out what it's all about. Nothing I've done in my near-40 years on this planet has been filled with such contrast.

Of course there are great highs: the limitless love, the sense of connection, the unmatched dedication to the point where you'd give your next breath. But there's also the sleep so broken your eyes feel bathed in acid, the questioning so deep because it revolves around a little human who's still part of you. These two sides of the story are woven together like threads on a quilt.

I think for a while I was confused, almost incredulous, that my friends hadn't clued me in to all this. No one took the time to explain the heart-expanding, ground-shaking change that a little one brings. But when I sit in front of a friend who is pregnant with their first baby I find it hard to explain, too.

You can't fully describe what it feels like to wake up a child each morning with a heart bursting with love, even though they have woken you up so many times you can no longer recall basic vocabulary.

I've experienced motherhood like a second adolescence. It has made me question every facet of who I am. This has been unexpected. I've always felt a capable person and I've wanted a child since I held my first doll at age five or six.

I coo annoyingly at babies in cafes, so I thought I would add one to the gang with ease. I imagined travelling around Burma with my newborn on maternity leave, him gurgling next to me as I cooked. In reality, I found going to the corner shop quite a big deal, for quite a few months.

For me, motherhood has been no joke. Blazing glory and heady joy combined with the lowest of lows. It wasn't until I read a passage in a book about postnatal depression that it all added up. My brain was out of balance, and I hadn't allowed myself the space to see what was happening.

How could I have seen – among the nappies, the bedtimes, the emails, the Instagram posts, the books and the business of what I do? What all women do? But it was there, and eventually it rose to the surface.

I'm proud to be a person who sees the positive in all situations, so for me this was a hard place to inhabit. Somehow I felt like these feelings – of sadness, of worthlessness, of incompetence – dampened the glow of my love for my son and the wonder of his being.

It took me a long time to be comfortable with the fact that these things were separate; that being a mother didn't mean I would always be bulletproof; and that feeling down was not a reflection on my love for my son. Not admitting it – that's the thing that is damaging

I have – with the support of my incomprehensibly patient, at times saintly, husband, supportive family and some incredible women and friends – been able to navigate it all.

I've begun to understand what happened and to be able to talk about it.

It astounded me to learn that one in four mothers suffer with postnatal depression in some way. I'm sure huge numbers more feel depleted and at times unable to cope.

Motherhood has opened me up. If I was only playing scales on one octave before, now I'm up and down the 88 keys and seven octaves every single day. My top notes are higher and my bass notes are lower.

With daily practice, the lows have become mere moments while the highs are symphonies stretching for far, far longer than before. I'll never be the same again, and I owe it to you, little Dylan, for teaching me more in your three years on this earth than any other being ever will.

I cherish every damn second, good or bad, because they are all making me the woman I never knew I could become.

Yomi Adegoke
Ana Santi
Olivia Sudjic
Sophie Wilkinson

WORKS OF
FICTION

YO
UN
G
LO
VE

SEPTEMBER
BABIES

Yomi Adegoke

*Yomi Adegoke is a journalist and the co-author of bestselling
Slay in Your Lane, a guide to life for black British women.
Young adult fiction is one of literature's most emotive genres –
replete with tales of self-discovery and first love. Here Yomi
writes about a teen romance that lasts longer than it should.*

David was loud. Annoyingly so, but by the time you told him to lower his voice, you were doing so through stifled laughter. His big mouth saved him as often as it got him into trouble. 'An absolute gobshite,' his mum would whisper to me, as he hollered in the distance.

We had both gone to Ecclesborne Manor from year seven – it was a grandly named, money-poor school (even the crappiest schools sound like elite country estates in England). He was laddish in a way that made me nervous; a boy who only seemed to acknowledge anyone outside of his friendship group to wind them up or wind them. We shared no classes then: his strongest subjects — IT, PE, maths – were my weakest, and where I flourished with words, he was always in bottom set.

David only truly saw me in year nine, when we were both bigger and broader. He was always tall for his age, and by 14 had gained the mass that saw him copping cigarettes for his more baby-faced friends. He sat across from me in physics and I'd feel his eyes and catch them just before he frantically caught himself.

For a while, we were only capable of communicating in insults or accusation. I was a 'snake' for not reminding him of our homework due date, he was a 'mong' for forgetting in the first place. 'You guys fancy each other,' his mates and mine would chime. 'Fuck off,' we'd say in unison, fuelling the fire.

By year 10, puberty had inoculated us against cooties. The act of signing in and out of MSN Messenger for attention had become delicate forehead kisses that left me melting, as my bumpy spots brushed against his lips. Dry humps to Ne-Yo.

Drunk on love and WKD and youth. We were September babies – both Virgos – which meant something, though I can't remember exactly what now. He told me he loved me on my 15th birthday and 12 days later, on his, we went all the way, promising we'd never return.

—

When David got sick, we'd been together all of eight months. But at 15 it was a pretty big portion of our existence. The word cancer was terrifying – a near-mythical, monstrous thing we'd raised thousands of pounds to 'beat'. Natalie's mum had it, and we had done a sponsored fun run in the summer. We couldn't believe someone at school actually had it, though.

Though we were all scared, David feigned courage. It was almost convincing. He liked to use the proper terminology – synovial sarcoma. He had it in his right lung, and seemed almost proud of its rarity. My mum, whose eyes began to glisten just thinking about David's mother, said I was an angel sent to watch over them. They were lucky to have me, she said; it could easily have been one of us.

I would do homework in snatches in hospital halls, sitting tentatively at his bedside after the surgery and chemotherapy and radiation. I only ever cried when he slept. He celebrated his 16th birthday on the children's ward, with an Arsenal cake he couldn't eat. For a year and a half, I watched as it took his hair and his girth and his smile. His eyes became watery and vacant, hooded by veiny lids, and his skin translucent. 'You look like Voldemort,' I'd joke. The energy it took him to attempt a smirk killed me.

I don't think the severity had sunk in for any of us, until the special assemblies. As soon as it was confirmed terminal, and the doctors gave David eight weeks to live, teachers, classmates, dinner ladies and parents began mourning him, as he seemed to slip in and out of our lives and life itself.

One early afternoon in spring, I bunked history to bring him Sin City. "Marry me," he said calmly as I put down my bag. "I've already asked your mum. I want to spend the rest of my life with you." I know now he got it from that Mandy Moore film, where she had leukemia and married a heartthrob in the Deep South just before she died. "Of course," I said through tears, as happy as they were sad.

Six days later, we were married. We picked a wedding dress and suit from Scope, my sister and my two best mates bridesmaids in Risky. We exchanged our vows in matching Nike TNs, our favourite song, Live Your Life by T.I., playing as we tearfully said our 'I do's'. The photographer was David's PE teacher and the reception was in our local pub. It was ridiculous and it was perfect. We were children, teetering at that time when you know nothing and so are immortal, fearless in the face of unknown.

—

It was about a year and a half before I realised that David was not going to die. Nine months after the date we were due to bury him, he was given the all-clear by doctors. They were cautious, but I knew. The more excited everyone became, the more it confirmed David had cheated death. And the more I felt cheated.

It sounds strange, this deepening dread. But his death was what all of us had prepared for. I was wearily accustomed to the idea I'd be a child bride and a teen widow before I could legally drink. I'd already grieved for the life we'd never get to share. I'd made plans. Plans in which he only featured as a memory; plans that would honour his memory. I was going to go to university, to get a good job. And someday find another husband – who wasn't David, but was still mine – who I'd love not more, but differently.

And I was already so different to how I had been at 16; we both were. David had put the weight back on and his hair had grown back, but the smile never returned. His jibes were no longer laced with facetiousness, his accusations now steeped in real insecurity. It's like the sickness had seeped through the lining of his body, pushed past the marrow of his bones and settled in his soul. He'd always been a bit of a prick – what 16-year-old boy isn't? – but years of suspended hope and resentment at missed milestones made him sour more than the illness ever could. The bile had to go somewhere.

So many of us worry about becoming our mothers, but I spent my late teens fretting I had become his. I cooked for him, cleaned for him, washed his pants. After our first baby she and I were indistinguishable – swinging breasts, sagging stomach and sunken eyes. He reminded me of my shortcomings on a daily basis, pitting me against a version of me I'm not sure ever existed.

People-watching became my hobby. I'd escape for hours in mundane Instagram feeds and Facebook wormholes, scrolling through the lives of those who left our town and did something, anything. At 26, most of our schoolmates weren't even close to marriage, a house, kids. They were too busy living a delayed adolescence I was sickened by and envious of.

I often wondered if he had actually changed at all, or if I'd been too in love or too young to notice how cruel he could be. Or maybe I'd changed. Or he'd died after all. Maybe we both had, and our endless, shitty marriage was our shared hell. Still, I pitied him almost as much as I pitied myself. "I want to spend the rest of my life with you," David had said, expecting his life to be over in a few short weeks.

—

At GCSE, I'd studied Romeo and Juliet and told David it was like the play was about us. It's only in hindsight you realise not just how fucking stupid they were, but also how it was largely because they were so fucking young.

Like them, we didn't know each other. We didn't know ourselves. I'd given him the best years of my life, what felt like the only years of my life, really. Imagine being permanently tied to the first boy who broke your heart, whose name almost escapes you and whose Facebook updates now make you gag.

David is loud. Annoyingly so. Infuriatingly so. But now his shouting is a constant, jolting reminder that I'm still here. Sometimes, in the rare moments I have to daydream, I imagine sneaking into our room as he sleeps and smothering him. I see the life leave him as it should have a decade ago, as a pillow quietens his struggle and puts him to sleep for good.

And for a brief moment, as I stare at this alternative reality where fate corrects itself, I feel myself smile.

MEMORY

THE
LIST

Ana Santi

Ana Santi is a journalist and editor-in-chief at Jigsaw. This is her first piece of fiction: a short story based on her childhood experience of moving from Brazil to England.

The setting for the ball was the landing. I don't remember playing there before, but there was something about the pink marbled floor and shiny black banister, with views over the spiral staircase, that felt right for the occasion. I'd chosen a silk emerald dress, cut long and straight by my seamstress grandmother from the lustrous scraps of her clients' outfits. My dolls were always the best dressed. I was trying to find some matching shoes when I heard the doorbell ring.

My gran called up to me. Reluctantly, I went downstairs and found my father, alone in the front garden under an umbrella. I walked as far as I could towards him without straying from the terrace. He knelt down, still under his umbrella (why wouldn't you shelter in the dry?), to talk to me. If he said anything else that day, I can't recall it; his visit seemed to last seconds and he didn't come past the garden, into the house. But I do remember this: he told me that if I didn't want to go to England I should take a piece of paper and draw two columns, one filled with reasons to stay, the other with reasons to go. Then he left, and I never saw him again.

I'm sitting on the floor of my bedroom at my parents' house in Devon, surrounded by empty boxes; only one remains unopened. Old photographs, postcards, homework, ticket stubs, letters, dissertations, a biography of Steffi Graf cover the carpet. Did I write the list? At eight years old, what would I have done with the choice? Did I even want one? I know it's there, but I can't find the memory. It was 30 years ago.

What I do remember is the plane journey from São Paulo to Heathrow on New Year's Eve, my sister and me sitting on the floor of the first middle row, playing games. My socks and sandals made me laugh. I'd never worn socks with sandals before, but I was yet to understand the need for boots. I think back to the screams, tears and anger when my mum told us, as we sat on her futon at my step-grandparents' house, that we weren't going back to Brazil, failing to understand (as no eight year-old should) her own tears and the complexities of the decisions made by a mother.

I remember refusing to go to school, a month later. Making a fuss over the uniform and missing out on the pleated skirt I secretly loved. Being unable to speak English. Overwhelmed by the attention – would you like to borrow my ruler? Will you play with us today? Can I sit next to you at lunch? Wishing I could change my surname to my dad's – my stepdad's, that is – so I could blend in, but too embarrassed (or guilty? To me, he was already my dad) to ask. Grateful for my pale skin.

Then, making proper friends. As part of a school project when I was 15, we had to create a newspaper and vote for the editor. "You should put yourself forward," said my friend. I shook my head. I was shy, never the centre of attention. "You really should," said another, more vocal classmate, as others agreed. I didn't realise they saw me in this way, as capable, a leader. So I put my hand up and when the vote was cast, I won. I picked reporters, sub and picture editors, a deputy. I asked for stories to be re-written, and they were. For better headlines and different pictures. I was running a team of 29 students, all working hard and having fun, united in making something excellent. And we did. I remember relishing being different. Proud that no one else could speak Portuguese.

Turning it into my job, years later. Reporting on the Brazilian fashion industry. Annoyed that I didn't tan better: you don't look South American! You don't have an accent! Rarely being recognised as Brazilian at all. Wondering if I'd left something behind.

I don't want to open the last box. Whatever is or isn't in there is bound to be disappointing. A rubbish, embarrassing list written by a child; a list I might have to evaluate as an adult. No list at all. A conclusion of some sort.

My sister pokes her head in to ask what I'm doing. When I tell her, she laughs. Because she remembers the list. Or rather, she remembers my annoyance at having to consider it, instead of hosting the ball. I left one column blank, she tells me, the one headed Why I Should Stay. In the other, I wrote one reason: because my mum and sister are going.

SOFT
HAIR

Olivia Sudjic

Olivia Sudjic is an author whose debut book, Sympathy, was hailed as the 'first great Instagram novel'. She's since published an essay on anxiety called Exposure. Soft Hair, featuring cats, quantum nanophysics and Cointreau, is her first short story.

I wanted to take a holiday to ignore the festive period but I didn't have the cash. It's expensive to meet the world on your own terms. It's expensive to be single. I decided I'd stay with friends instead but not one of them invited me, which put an end to that. Then I decided what I needed was just to get out of my flat. To live somewhere new for a bit. Maybe I could be the guardian of someone's left-behinds. Pets abandoned over Christmas. I hate animals – unpredictable – but made a few enquiries. A friend of a friend knew someone skipping town until mid-January, two cats requiring company confined indoors. Someone masochistic, really, only there to be ignored.

When I was young my mother let two artists stay in our home while we tried out various cults. When we returned they'd cut down our trees. Spoiled the view, the girlfriend said. Another year we went to house-sit for a woman my mother barely knew. The woman was supposed to be going away, but never did. We became something like her maids that summer, the two of us making meals and hanging laundry. I thought of these experiences and my fear of cats for several days as I decided what to do. Fairy lights appeared on neighbouring balconies. The man next door had his whole façade lit and twinkling. Then I heard him screaming, swearing nonstop for about 90 minutes. I'd often worried he was abusing a silent person and hoped he was watching a silent game. Then the man went down into the stairwell screaming. "Yes," I texted, "where to find the keys?"

On the doorstep, Christmas Eve, I paused to take a breath. I was now a 36-year-old research fellow in quantum nanophysics. I had no need to fear a pair of pampered house cats. Still, I was judicious opening the door. I slunk into the hallway and shut it swiftly behind, placing both my bags on the floor. Some places I go in and think 'yes'. Others the feeling is 'no'. I'd guessed from the street which way it would go, that these were people who lived differently. There were photographs to prove it, hung from every vertical plane and propped on every horizontal. From the repeat appearances I discerned the owners' faces, a couple younger than me. There were photographs of the cats as well. Expensively framed A3 portraits. Then I noticed an oil painting above the mantelpiece of a solitary bride, the woman from the photos, whose house keys I now held in my hand.

Lengthy instructions had been typed, printed and left on the marble kitchen counter. As I read (rubbish bins, a cleaner, tricks to tell the cats apart) something brushed my leg. It jumped up and sprawled across the papers. Imperious gaze identical to its expression on the wall. Having no second cat to compare, I don't know why I assumed it was the female. I suppose it felt less threatening than to be alone in proximity to a male. It followed me as I went exploring, into every bathroom cupboard to inspect their pills and toiletries before unpacking.

The cats, white Himalayans, appeared wherever I sat, like puffballs in a forest. I say cats. It seemed to be the same cat each time, or I never saw the two cats in the same moment. The boy cat must have been hiding, and fair enough. It was normal to be put out by home invaders, especially when you were held in captivity. The girl cat leapt onto the bed, her thousand-yard stare fixed beyond the window. I followed it to where two ring-necked parakeets sat, bright green in the bare branches. She watched the lovebirds with murderous desire and something about the intensity – the privacy – of this moment caught me off guard. I stroked her experimentally. As I did, great clouds of fur rose into the air, like silver steam inside the sunlight. The cat didn't appear to notice, accepting how my hand followed her spine as if this were its sole duty. I tried different things, touching under her chin, behind her ears, feeling the softness of her belly. I looked into her eyes, unable to recall a time I'd been this bold in my affections.

After a few hours I became uneasy. Surely the male cat was curious? Was it lurking somewhere, watching? The fur of the first was webbed all over my body, perhaps he was feeling jealous. I got down on my hands and knees and prowled around the house. From this vantage point, low to the ground, I could see how thickly cat hair lay, a sheen on the carpet. Now I'd turned away from her, she came after me. Nuzzling at my flank, probing with her head, investigating my investigations with a rough pink tongue.

I thought then, on all fours, of Stephen Hawking's paper, completed in the last days before he died. What happens when a black hole evaporates? What happens to everything inside? It goes, partly, into soft hair. "A haze of photons at the event horizon, a black hole's point of no return." Was it possible the second cat had fled the instant I'd entered his prison? Perhaps it had been waiting on the mat and slipped out between my legs or beneath the heft of my two bags. I shook the treats, poking into every hiding place with rising panic. The first cat watched over my indignity from the counter like the Sphinx.

I shut the existing cat in the bedroom, paws scrabbling wildly in protest like my heart against its cage. I seemed to spread disorder. I suspected my internal chaos, the entropy of my life, to be contaminant. It didn't matter where I went, it came with me, stuck to me, then began to shed. With one cat locked away I crept again around the house. Perhaps it was moving between hiding places. My skin burned. That itchy feeling that means hives are coming, as if my skin's been wrapped in burlap. I went back to the woman's instructions, to the friend's text. To check I wasn't imagining the second cat I studied the photographs. Two for sure. Besides, one cat could not produce so much hair.

I took the keys and went into the street in my soft white socks. Up and down in the freezing cold, the windows shining with Christmas trees, each decorated in the same tasteful scheme. The houses here all aspired to the same life. I shook my treats in desperation. It would be dark soon. But I couldn't knock on doors and speak to strangers. I wasn't ready for that.

A sound. A cat sound. A covered motorbike parked inside the low wall of a neighbour's property caught my eye. I stooped, trembling, to lift its silver cover. A cat, white Himalayan, its eyes a piercing blue, squinted and shrank into the crawlspace beneath the engine. I was afraid of his cunning and his claws, his evident disdain, but more afraid he would disappear, again, and so adrenaline took over. I grabbed one paw and dragged him out from under, hissing and spitting at me.

I threw the disappearing cat down inside the hall, shut the door, then lay on the polished floor breathing heavily. One came to nose me over. I felt the second climb on top, frisking my lower half. It sounded as if more paws came trotting down the stairs; there seemed to be paws all over. I submitted, wondering if I could enjoy this form of touch, if I might, through this, become a cat person. I stared at the portrait of the bride, blonde hair framing feline eyes. Cat pair, bird pair, person pair – I was still me, unbelonging on the floor. I felt very far from home then. From the life I might've had, or the life I'd wanted. I got up and stood over the mirrored drinks trolley, catching my own reflection.

I'd never tried Cointreau. Not knowingly. On the few occasions I'd found myself at student bars I'd ordered Babycham because my mother drank it. But no sooner had I clasped the amber bottle than I watched it slip from me in excruciatingly slow motion. The glass smashed everywhere while I stood frozen. Three white, collarless cats, identical blue eyes and flat noses, glared at me. The sickly smell of oranges overpowering.

I still think about the one I eventually chose to put outside. The quantum cat with its soft hair all matted and sticky. And I hope it's the interloper who lives there now since I played god; my little winter remedy.

OGRES & GOOD GUYS: A STORY FOR MY NEPHEWS

Sophie Wilkinson

Sophie Wilkinson is a journalist and scriptwriter specialising in culture and society. Often, she's commissioned to cover women's issues for women readers. Here she changes tack and writes a fairytale for her nephews, with lessons for them to grow up with.

Once upon a time, the oldest of you was born, on the same wintry night that Barack Obama, a man who'd talked on his campaign trail about women being as deserving as men, became the first black US president. Once upon a more recent time, another one of you was born, just a few days before tennis player Andy Murray became the first British man to win Wimbledon in 77 years. Andy would sternly correct reporters who said his achievements were pioneering, reminding those men of the women who'd done it first, and would go on to work with a woman as his coach. And once upon a very recent time, the youngest of you was born, in the scorching summer that Mad Max: Fury Road was released. While promoting the film, actor Tom Hardy said women – like his co-star Charlize Theron – could do anything he could, arguing the case for "better parts for women than just girlfriend and wife or lover … because I'm bored with that".

Though so much of history has been built and told by ogres – nasty men who proudly lock women away so they can't realise their true potential – each of you arrived in the world at times when some of the most powerful, respected and talented men out there declared that women deserve equality. They and many others – the good guys – dream of a future in which women get to live outside cold, isolating towers. More than that, they're striving for a world in which women get a chance to catch up on what they've missed while being cruelly locked up. These men are looking out for your sisters.

When I talk about your sisters, by the way, I mean your literal sisters: the one who was born the same autumn that the Equality Act, signed off by a majority-male parliament, came into force; the one who arrived the day Gareth Southgate's England men's football team bowed out of their best performance in decades, a tournament punctuated with affection and empathetic feedback from their leader.

I also mean the sisters who walk with you in life: your mothers, your teachers, your friends, your future colleagues, mentors, superiors, acquaintances and the women you may one day love dearly. (While you don't need any sort of connection to a woman to be able to respect them, I'd question the happiness of any boy or man who had none.)

Anyway, these good guys and all the women they stood up for are now in trouble, because the ogres sought revenge. The women are being flung back into their towers, and so many of the good guys – ready to find their place in a bright new land where the neediest are helped first – have instead been exiled into wilderness. The ogres are threatened by women's voices, by hands shaking across borders, by the gentle, impressive power of just making friends and having conversations.

They've demanded the world be tailored to their greeds and petty fears, and are so aware of their own terribleness that they're trying to rewrite history to make themselves look better. They want you to think they're the real victims here, and that the good guys are the bad guys, and that all the women deserved to be in those towers all along.

My darling, soft-cheeked nephews, I don't want you to end up like those ogres, all mean and scared. You're the sweetest boys I've ever known and deserve to grow up to be the good guys. If the ogres keep getting their way, though, your sisters will grow up in towers. They will be told to dress in the finest colours, patterns and fabrics, but only if they follow a long list of unwritten, whispered rules. Get one thing wrong, and they'll be teased and blamed. Follow the rules too closely, and they'll also be teased and blamed.

They will work harder than you but not be taken as seriously as you. They will be paid less than you, especially if they become mummies. They will be at risk of violence from all sorts of ogres – obvious, hideous ogres, and then the ogres who seem kind and gentle at first but are really, deep down, the nastiest creatures alive. They will be encouraged to become invisible.

If the ogres keep getting their way, you boys will be relegated to the wilderness, to fend for yourself. You'll be told you don't have to work hard to get results, but that work is your only cause. You'll be encouraged to retreat into yourself, to replace your feelings with a brittle, patchy armour. You'll be pressured to hunt for success at all costs.

Demands will be made in small ways every day, for you to do things you don't know how to do. You'll stop smiling, because looking approachable means looking weak, and beauty isn't something you're allowed to have for yourself. You'll be told to treat your sisters like things, not humans. And if you ever so much as hug another man, you'll both turn to stone.

That ogre life sounds totally rubbish, doesn't it? However, with some magic powers, surely the ogres can be defeated.

Your lives are only beginning, and I'm not quite at the middle of my own. I can't pretend to know how all our stories will end. But if I could pick out any magic powers to help defeat those gruesome ogres, these are the 10 I would give you:

1. Listen as much as you speak.

2. Treat your sisters the same as you would like to be treated, because they aren't so different from you at all.

3. OK, there are some differences – I've supervised enough of your bath-times to have heard you each declare them matter-of-factly. But you won't allow these differences to make you think it's OK to hurt, exploit and leave women behind. That has been, is, and always will be, ogreish nonsense.

4. Look into your anger, to be able to wonder if another feeling, that you shouldn't be scared of, could take anger's place instead.

5. Tend to your emotions like you would a garden. Even if you try to swallow it down, that burning lump in your throat that pops up when you should be crying won't just disappear. Its seed will bury deep inside your tummy, and you never know what might end up growing out of it.

6. Sharpen your mind. It's your strongest weapon, and gets more powerful when it rubs up against new experiences, new stories, new conversations with new people from new places.

7. Treat the internet as a stepping stone – to use it to improve your life, not detract from it. Test how you feel with and without it.

8. Respect the choices of others. If a girl is allowed to do everything a boy is allowed to do, you don't need to judge her for something you could get away with.

9. When you're old enough, ask me what Mad Max: Fury Road is so we can watch it together.

10. Remember, above everything, that I'd give all the exact same magic powers to your sisters.

If all these magic powers work, and I hope they do, then our happily-ever-afters won't be so hard to reach.

Irenosen Okojie
Zing Tsjeng
Vicky Spratt
Sophie Mackintosh
Charlie Brinkhurst-Cuff

NEW GROUND
& BIG IDEAS

NOCTURNAL ZONES AND DISSIDENT WOMEN

Irenosen Okojie

Irenosen Okojie is a Nigerian-British writer who has published a collection of short stories and a prize-winning novel. She loves cinema, but has never written about it before. Here she looks at the power of female protagonists in three life-changing films.

There are certain films you carry with you long after you've finished watching. You might be familiar with the feeling of being utterly changed, yet unable to define exactly how. It's like an epiphany that comes in the form of a fog rather than a shining light. The sensation often comes late at night – after you've been watching films to combat insomnia, eating snacks the equivalent of your body weight, drinking rum concoctions with Irish cream to take the edge off.

I went through a period of watching films deep in the heart of the night, during an uncertain period in my life where I felt somewhat disconnected from the outside world and unsure of my place within it. I was finding my way with my writing, trying to define who I was as an artist, reaching blindly in the dark for clues. To try to shake myself out of it, I deliberately sought out films that pivoted away from the standard presentations of women – or what women should aspire to be. The dissident women I connected with taught me about storytelling – about how to be a better artist.

The first time I saw The Double Life of Veronique directed by Polish auteur Krzysztof Kieslowski, I wept. The film stars the luminous Irene Jacob as the characters of Veronique and Weronika, and it charts the parallel stories of two identical women – one in Poland, the other in France. They're unaware of one another's existence but their lives profoundly intersect. It traverses the themes of love, identity and intuition. The two women share an intriguing bond transcending language and geography.

From its cleverly varied operatic score and meditative moments, to the random encounters between characters that may or may not have some deeper meaning, the experience of watching the film is like touching a cosmic consciousness. In one scene, Veronique spots a puppeteer while driving home at night. A few days later she starts to feel the strange absence of a great loss, and then receives a letter with a shoelace inside. Later still, she discovers that same puppeteer she saw is a children's book writer who has written several books, one about a shoelace.

Kieslowski's film changed me on a profound level. I walked around in a stupor for days afterwards, drunk on its ethereal quality and its tale of the intriguing ways we're drawn to certain individuals, as though they're destined to leave a mark on us. The film went on to impact the shape of my first novel. It showed me that time and storytelling didn't have to be linear; it showed me the wonder of creating threads between worlds that on the surface might appear far removed from each other.

Equally influential, Lynne Ramsay's mesmeric Morvern Callar follows a young supermarket stacker called Morvern through a remote Scottish town. On Christmas morning, she wakes up to find her boyfriend has died by suicide. She then chops his body up into pieces, buries them, takes his cash card, claims the manuscript of his first novel as her own and sends it to a publisher. She receives a large advance and goes off on holiday to Spain with her best friend.

With an enigmatic and startling central performance from the terrific Samantha Morton, the film is a fascinating exploration of grief, of our expectations for how women are supposed to behave when they mourn. It occurred to me for the first time that female characters don't have to be likable in a traditional sense. Society conditions us to feel we have to be nice, pliable and pretty not only to survive but to thrive. But niceness can be crippling for women. Here was a character who put herself first, who was selfish. Was she in shock? Could she be described as cold-blooded? Or was she experiencing an awakening? I learned you could make female characters dark and devious if you gave them layers of complexity. I was blown away by Ramsay's daring and her stark refusal to make the character palatable to a mainstream audience.

Last but not least, Spike Lee's seminal debut film She's Gotta Have It had a deep and liberating effect on me. His protagonist, the gorgeous Nola Darling played by Tracy Camilla Johns, juggles three lovers and the ups and downs of an artist's life in Brooklyn. The world opened up while I watched it. Here was a black female protagonist who subverted conventional perceptions of race and sexuality. Nola didn't shrink herself for the white gaze, nor apologise to the black gaze for fear of judgment or disapproval. She owned her sexuality in a way that was full-bodied and beautiful.

At the time, there were so few depictions of black women in this light, if any. Lee is so rarely given credit for it, but really what he did with this film was spearhead a new wave of American independent film-making. Through Nola, he focused on black women and made us complicated, gave us choices – a privilege we are so rarely afforded. Lee showed black bodies making love, and the capturing of Nola is tender, at once intimate and political. Nola's free spirit and Lee's free-wheeling artistic approach made for an indelible cinematic experience which resonated with me as a creative black woman. In short, this film made me feel seen.

The women in all these films were outliers. They were more authentic to me, less encumbered by society's expectations. They defined themselves for themselves alone, embraced their specific ideas of freedom, pursued what they wanted and gave of themselves in equal measure. They took risks, made questionable decisions, and then lived with the consequences. They were liberated, sensual and surprising. They were human.

At a time when I was questioning my own creative output, these provocative films shifted my perceptions of art, womanhood and the tenuous boundaries of a patriarchal system. They remain endlessly mysterious – lodged deep inside me – balancing exquisitely just beyond my reach. I like to think of them as waiting for me to know them all over again, in ways that are challenging and new.

COMFORT FOOD

Zing Tsjeng

*Zing Tsjeng is the UK editor of Broadly, VICE's digital platform
for women, and the author of the Forgotten Women book series.
Although raised by a mother with a profound love of food, Zing
has never written about her culinary heritage. Here, she looks at
what food can teach us about home.*

My mother taught me to eat. Not the guilt trips or diet tips that my friends received from their parents; my mother introduced me to lard, butter, marbled pork belly, dark chocolate and sugar. She first learned about food working as a cook in a French restaurant while studying in Ontario. She spent her weekends making omelettes by the dozen, and was taught to separate lettuce by throwing it at a wall. She remained the exact same size throughout: five foot five, with prescription glasses and straight black hair that reached all the way down her back.

I, on the other hand, was tubby throughout primary school in Singapore – chubby enough to merit entry to the government-run Trim and Fit programme, which everyone privately called the Trim and Fat Club. It meant I spent recess running around the football field in midday heat, a fate that condemned my less sturdy classmates to heatstroke and asthma attacks.

It didn't deter me from eating, thank god. All my memories of being a kid revolve around food. In the school canteen, I experimented by combining white rice and baked beans with spicy, stir-fried morning glory. I lost a baby tooth to an apple, which I finished eating even after I bled all over it. My mum encouraged me. After school, she ferried me to drama class and bought me chocolate cake with an orange Capri-Sun chaser. She gave me pockets of small change to buy tiny paper cups of Milo from vending machines, all so I could savour the intensely sweet chocolate residue at the bottom.

Every Sunday evening, she got takeaway for the family – styrofoam boxes of glazed soy sauce chicken, sauteed kai lan greens, and silky shrimp dumplings. She laughed when she saw the chicken bones pile up on my plate, and said approvingly as I peeled off fatty chicken skin to eat whole: 'The skin is the best part.' Her own family had lived through hunger in the Second World War; her oldest sister still remembers the indignation of their one boiled egg served to the only boy in the family. My mum sometimes complained about her own cholesterol and high blood pressure, but the indirect message only encouraged me – youth, she seemed to say, was for eating.

My mother introduced me to tonkatsu, a full decade before katsu became better known as a limp chicken cutlet in curry sauce served to overworked Brits at train stations. She taught me how to ask for the bill – an imperious, commanding wave – that works even in restaurants you can't quite afford. We ate olive rice and pomelo salad at a Thai cafe hidden behind a private swimming pool; grilled kaya toast with salted butter at a Hainanese coffee shop; and fresh popiah spring rolls of shredded jicama and egg at the rundown shopping mall opposite our house.

When I moved to London by myself, I left the Thai cafe and Hainanese coffee shop behind. Eating out – an everyday and affordable pleasure for most Singaporeans – was suddenly prohibitively expensive. My mother would return to her chef roots when she visited me. 'Do you want something to eat?' she'd text. By the time I turned up, there would be four or five dishes on the table.

Sometimes it would be comfort food: Chinese steamed egg, chicken curry and braised vegetables. Other dinners would be more adventurous. Thai eggplants stewed with chilli. Grilled skate with sambal. Fat, juicy deep-fried prawns dredged in salted egg for extra flavour. It was a good night when she served all five. 'I can't cook back in Singapore,' she sighed, waving me off when I thanked her. 'It's just too hot.'

The last time I saw her back home, we took my partner to stand in an hour-and-a-half-long queue for a bowl of noodles. The springy bak chor mee (Hokkien for 'meat noodles') at Hill Street Tai Hwa Pork Noodle comes in a chilli and vinegar sauce with the depth charge of a nuclear submarine. The street food stall was given a Michelin star in 2016. A bowl only cost £3.50, so we bought an extra one to share, plus a scallion pancake to tide us over in the queue. We laughed as the tourists dropped out, one by one, ahead of us.

One of the greatest gifts a mother can give her daughter is teaching her to eat ravenously. We raise girls to be ladylike and proper: to chew with their mouth shut, to count their calories and pose with salads. But eating, by its very nature, is not ladylike. This is why as many girls as possible should try to enjoy it. The masticating gums, the crunch and swallow, the churn of your gut – all of it is visceral, bloody, glorious. It is also a universal necessity and bodily function – but only one gender is looked upon so unfavourably for indulging in it.

I feel unspeakably lucky to have been raised in the glorious tradition of makan ('eating' in Malay), in a multilingual country that hums with a dozen different dialects and a slush pile cuisine of every other country in south-east Asia and beyond. I have never drunk a diet shake, barring a disastrous encounter with reviewing a liquid diet at a fashion magazine. I don't think a meal tastes right without carbs, and I was almost driven to tears when a friend ordered a main in a Chinese restaurant without rice.

School friends used to call me the human rubbish bin on account of the way I hoovered up leftovers. You might think the nickname cruel, but I found it endearing. To me, wasting food is a sin, similar to skipping meals or wanting to subsist entirely on Huel. Who wouldn't want to be a food bin, tasting all the scraps of everyone else's delicious meals, sampling the widest variety of human cuisine possible? Food is a form of culture. Unlike art, music, or cinema, it is the only art form that you can quite literally devour.

People build personalities on being foodies. They take pride in describing dishes as 'umami' or knowing which chef has gone where. They attend specialist food markets and follow pop-ups that have their own Instagram accounts. My mum, who has never knowingly followed a food blogger on social media, doesn't dress up her love of food in fancy language or glossy image posts. Things either taste good or they don't.

The idea of home is a little more complicated. Physically speaking, you can only ever be home or away from home, but food blurs this divide. It turns your homesickness into a liminal state in which a familiar smell has the power to transport you across oceans and continents. When I close my eyes after a spoonful of my mum's steamed egg in London, I'm not literally back in Singapore. But something on a deeper level – my vibrating tastebuds, the salty aroma in my nostrils – has never been more at home.

DARE
TO
DO

Vicky Spratt

As a journalist, Vicky Spratt has led campaigns including Make Renting Fair, which succeeded in getting letting fees banned in England. Her first book, Tenants, is about the housing crisis and will be out in 2020. It might be easy to criticise political systems; it's harder to dream of what a better world might look like. Here, Vicky gives it a shot.

Knowledge is supposed to increase with age. In some ways, I guess, it's true. I'm 30 now. I know it's a bad idea to spend more than you earn, exceed two glasses of wine at an event you don't really want to be at and pursue people who never text back. I've also finally accepted that exercise really is the only way to stay feeling balanced. The paradox, though, is that the older I get, the more comfortable I am with everything I don't know.

It feels like so much of the world is back to front and upside down. You can go to the supermarket and for less than a fiver buy a whole chicken that's never seen the light of day, but the trains that take people from their homes to their jobs are totally unaffordable. Not a month goes by without an apocalyptic climate change warning, and yet as you scroll through the stories about it you're bombarded with cheap Ryanair and EasyJet flights which, let's face it, you want to book. Politicians seem to speak in a code designed only for each other despite spending 90% of their time insisting that they are 'for the people'. And, the tiny phones we carry around with us everywhere are a million times faster than the Nasa computer that first guided a man to the moon, but there are still millions of people living in poverty.

It would actually be easier to ask why things are the way they are – and talk about ways to make the world fairer – than it is to perform the acrobatic cognitive dissonance that we all do in order to pretend that everything's OK. But here we are, keeping on keeping on. I'm worried about climate change, but I bought fast fashion in the January sales because 'one woman boycotting the high street won't change anything, will it?'

It's so seductive. Who doesn't want to believe that the answers to difficult questions lie elsewhere?

The older I get the more I see the dangers of the stories we've been told about knowledge and power. It's 'weak' when a politician changes their mind and 'does a U-turn'; not having the answers is a sign of fragility or, worse, stupidity, and so nobody is prepared to say: 'I don't know but let's figure it out.'

Everywhere, in all the corners of our lives, there are people using their platform to say they have the answers. What's the secret of eternal youth? Definitely a vampire facial. How do you stop feeling like you're walking around with a miasma of malaise hanging over you all the bloody time? Marie Kondo the shit out of everything, obviously. Is the planet about to die? Not if you, yes you, go vegan right now.

And, for so many of us, with our demanding jobs, strained bank balances, young children, ageing parents, sapping hangovers and friends in need, these quick fixes represent time-saving solutions.

It's not a stretch to see how Brexit represents that for some people, too. Not making enough money, unhappy with your lot, worried about immigration? Brexit will fix it. Brexit is shorthand for a thousand different things. It means everything and it means nothing. It means whatever you want it to mean.

At school, I dreaded physics lessons. The equations needed to understand how our world is (probably) put together made my brain feel like snapping elastic. I wanted to ask so many questions. How do we know everything is made of atoms? Why can't we see them spilling like marbles when something breaks, then? Is your soul made of them, too? Do we even have souls? I'd fixate on all the things I didn't know. When we got to the solar system, I really struggled. What do you mean we don't really know why we're here? Are you seriously telling me matter is unpredictable?

Eventually, I asked one out loud.

"But, what happens after Pluto?"

My teacher said: "We don't really know, but to pass your exam you need to say Pluto is definitely the last planet."

The cat was out of the bag. Adults – parents, teachers, people in positions of authority – don't always have the answers. You don't turn 25, 30, 40 or 50 and suddenly just know.

In January 2019, Nasa received a signal from its New Horizons probe as it passed a large icy mass known as Ultima Thule. It's way out in space, beyond Pluto, among a collection of hundreds of thousands of frozen bits of galactic clutter orbiting the sun. I thought of physics class.

That probe set off when I was still at school, before people used iPhones or Tinder. It has travelled steadily through space, sending home grainy information on its way to tell us there's still an infinitude of stuff we don't know.

Spacecraft have never ventured so far beyond what we know. Ultima, it turns out, might just hold the clues to the conditions in which our solar system was initially forged 4.6 billion years ago and it's taken us 13 years to reach them.

After emerging from the primordial ooze of early adulthood I find it hard to trust people who are sure about everything because most of life is clearly trial and error. There is rarely one solution, seldom an easy answer. In my work now I often ask what a better world might look like. Who has the answer, the left or the right? What or where is modern Utopia? The headline-unworthy answer, always, is that there's no definitive version of Utopia but instead lots of ideas we need to be brave enough to try. We won't know if they'll work until we do and, along the way, they might fail and force us to change course.

I don't know exactly what Utopia looks like but I know it doesn't look like the world we live in now. Sure, most people can access Facebook and dating apps, which is great and everything, but wealth inequality is growing. Having 500 Facebook friends won't help you pay your rent.

Universal basic income? Let's do it and see if it works instead of arguing about all the reasons why it won't. Ditto safe and affordable housing for everyone, re-nationalised trains, cutting our meat consumption in a meaningful way, and having serious conversations about the environmental impact of fast fashion – no matter how uncomfortable it makes us.

We shouldn't be Pollyannaish about life. Blind optimism implies a few pink placards on a march will make everything OK. Equally, pure pessimism suggests you can't make a difference. Both are, in their own way, excuses for inaction.

Newsflash: you can't fix climate change or end any kind of inequality overnight. Change is incremental.

The internet has lulled us all into a false sense of security. It gives us the feeling that everything is accounted for, and is therefore transparent. If we've learned anything since 2016, it's that this simply isn't true. There are always invisible forces with vested interests at work. We inhabit giant structures designed to keep us nervous, cynical, selfish and disengaged.

At university, I had a crisis of confidence in my ability to answer difficult questions. I'll never forget what my tutor said to me then: "It's not about what you don't know, it's about what you do know."

Utopia, by its nature, might always be just out of reach, but that doesn't mean we shouldn't embrace the knowledge we do have and dare to dream about what it might look like.

Whenever I find myself fixating on what I don't know now, I think of being told to write that there were no planets after Pluto, not because it was true but because it would get me a GCSE. Then I think about the fact that people used to think the Earth was flat. Some people still do.

Don't worry about being perfect. You can always be better. Is Utopia even achievable personally or politically anyway? Don't worry about about having all the answers. Just commit to asking difficult questions, and always beware simple solutions to complex problems.

If all that's certain is uncertainty, we must have two constants: curiosity and hope.

ATTEMPTS AT DOMESTICITY

Sophie Mackintosh

Sophie Mackintosh made the Man Booker longlist in 2018 with her dystopian debut, The Water Cure. While writing head-turning fiction is in her remit, being tidy is not. Here she tackles her 'embarrassing' failure at domesticity, and unpacks the gendered pressure around keeping a home.

A couple of times a month I find myself Googling the question: does anyone else find keeping their house clean overwhelming? I read long threads on forums from women – they're always women – who have a difficult time keeping everything the way they feel it should be. Often these women have family and pets, which I don't. Other times I read descriptions of their mess and realise their mess is not what I would call mess – that we are operating on different levels. Those posts don't make me feel better. Occasionally I do find a descriptor of what I'm like, though – small untidinesses accumulating, stuff on the table where we eat our dinner, plates left overnight (or longer), clothes strewn over the bannister, dust just not really thought about, until suddenly everything seems terrible. I know then that I'm not alone.

I've tried many things to become a tidy person. For a while I obsessively read minimalist blogs, getting rid of most of my things (clothes and books excepting). This helped, except I live with someone else, and I'm not about to throw out their beloved things for my own happiness. I read cleaning blogs and tips and life-hacks and Instagram accounts, and made conscious efforts to develop tidy habits. I'm getting better, slowly but surely, learning these tricks that feel like they come so naturally to everyone else. But it's a matter of steps forward and steps back. The mess can feel malevolent, something building in the hours when I'm asleep.

In every other area of my life, just about, I feel like I have it together – at least superficially. I'm a published author. I teach and give talks to roomfuls of people. I can cook fancy dinners, go for long runs and do my taxes. I can fix washing machines

and assemble furniture and read maps. I'd be OK surviving in
the wilderness for about three days, as a ballpark figure.

But sometimes, when someone drops by unexpectedly –
whether family or our letting agency, friends or strangers –
I can have a panic attack at the idea of them seeing my flat,
and the mess that encroaches as soon as I let my guard down.
Sometimes I just don't feel safe or comfortable in my own
space, and it feels like it's largely my own fault.

Shame is one of my most frequent emotions nowadays, newly
in my 30s, and still so undomestic, untidy, still a slattern. As
a teenager and in my 20s I gave myself grief for being messy
in other ways. My room reflected my life. Clothes lived on
the floor (or bed, scooted to one side when I decided to sleep).
An ocean of plates and shoes and books. Everything felt
temporary. I revelled in the messiness, believing I had more
important things to do than hoovering and mopping.

In another flat now, renting for several years, something's
changed. Perhaps part of the problem is that it's hard to find
the energy to dust when your home is a sort of stopgap, one
that hasn't seen any paint or love or maintenance for years.
Being houseproud feels beyond me sometimes. There's a
growing part of me that wants to do things like lovingly
wipe down a mid-century sideboard I found at an antiques
shop, or mop a kitchen floor that I have chosen myself to my
own design scheme. But I don't own furniture, have never
decorated a room. I do my best with what I have.

Instagram can be a dangerous place in this state of shame.
I follow London-dwellers living in houseplant-filled, calm

spaces, with stripped floorboards and tasteful lighting, and find myself enviously speculating about how they live that way. On very low days I think that maybe I'm just not good enough for that kind of life, when the reality is I'm just another victim of London's housing market.

But there are days when the shame leaves me for a while, and I do feel an affection towards this shambolic home. It's the first place I lived with the love of my life. It's cosy in the evenings, when the dust and subsidence cracks aren't visible. Still, when my parents visit, my mum gently suggests a cleaner. Their eyes go to where the carpet is pulling up at the edges. And the shame whooshes back in like a wave.

Sometimes this shame pulls me into existential zones. How could I have a baby, for example, when babies create exponential mess just by existing? How could I ever own a house and juggle life, upkeep, when I'm completely hopeless? Being messy becomes bigger than me; it becomes a moral indictment, a statement about what a failure I am.

I often work from home. I laugh darkly at the idea I had when I started: that my flat would be the cleanest it's ever been. Instead I'm a small tornado, scattering crumbs and paper everywhere, leaving the bed unmade and losing things.

More and more I think perhaps the key problem is that there are so often things that feel more urgent than a perfectly clean home. Like finishing my novel, or meeting a deadline, or pitching an article. Meeting friends, cooking lavish meals and in the process using every plate and bowl. Living a tidy life needs to be a priority, and until I fully embrace this over other priorities I know it will always be a struggle. In the meantime I'll try to improve, but I'll be kind to myself as well.

I'll aim to clean the sink last thing at night, but I won't sweat the under-the-sofa dust (not immediately, at least). I'll understand that it's a kind of gendered pressure, even when it comes from myself.

And I'll remember that ignoring the mess helped my book get written, and I'll be grateful for that – grateful for the space that may not be perfect, but which is mine.

PSY
CHO
LO
GY

ON
NARCISSISM

Charlie Brinkhurst-Cuff

Charlie Brinkhurst-Cuff is the deputy editor of gal-dem, a magazine written by women of colour for all to explore, and the author of Mother Country: Real Stories of the Windrush Children. She has always been intrigued by narcissism, and takes a deep dive into the personality disorder here.

When I started researching narcissism, I wasn't expecting to find that it affects women more than men. I mean, just look at the political sphere. Male narcissists are everywhere: some of them have orange-gold tans – like evil little cheese puffs – and make decisions that benefit their ego without much regard for anyone else.

But the true story of narcissism is about women, because women are more likely to be the victims of narcissistic behaviour.

A person who is a narcissist can be defined by their ego and self-absorption. In our age of social media and selfies, the term is often thrown at millennials and Generation Z. Many of us go through periods of self-confidence where our ego is inflated, perhaps by likes and shares, which you could argue is narcissistic behaviour. But there is a difference between healthy narcissism, of which we all need a pinch, and narcissism that harms other people.

When a psychiatrist calls someone a narcissist, they are often talking about someone with narcissistic personality disorder (NPD). Their narcissism is essential and unchangeable and, according to experts, their narcissistic traits add up pathologically. Among other things, they lack empathy, are prone to sadism and need constant admiration. "What makes these traits a true personality disorder is that they take over people's lives and cause significant problems," explained social psychologist W. Keith Campbell in a 2016 TED talk.

It's not known what causes NPD, but as with other mental health disorders, there are complex factors involved, including upbringing ("excessive adoration or excessive criticism that is poorly attuned to the child's experience"), genetics and neurobiology. Unfortunately, studies have illustrated that little is known about the neurobiology of this disorder. However, one study on the cognitive neuroscience of NPD said: "There are consistencies pointing to abnormalities in certain brain areas, especially the insular cortex, that are associated with features of NPD, especially lack of empathy."

While people often self-diagnose anxiety and depression, narcissism is a trait we like to diagnose in others. You'll find reams of articles, quizzes and videos aimed at helping women identify whether their partner is a narcissist.

A year on from a break-up, I found myself knee-deep in this content, nodding red-eyed as I listened to Dr Ramani Durvasula, a psychologist based in the capital of narcissism, Los Angeles, explain that narcissists were hypersensitive to criticism and believed "the world never really got their greatness". This ex-boy of mine couldn't be happy for other people's successes and projected that feeling quite openly whenever something went well with my career. Textbook narcissism, I thought. He checks almost every box.

Initially, I worried that while calling my ex a narcissist was giving me a greater understanding of the person who wronged me, it would be unfair to give him such a stigmatised label. As a society we tend to conflate serious mental health conditions with personality traits. Are we too quick to jump and call people narcissists when narcissism can be pathological? However, Keeley Taverner, a psychologist who specialises in treating the victims of narcissistic behaviour, thinks it's good that people are increasingly aware of narcissistic traits and points out that narcissism isn't a mental health condition in the same way that anxiety or depression is those with narcissistic traits tend to benefit from them. "People were totally in the dark. They didn't have a clue and thought they were going loopy," she told me.

She's talking about many of her female patients, who are empaths, individuals highly attuned to other people's emotions. "Your narcissistic individual needs their polar opposite. Which is often highly sensitive, kind, considerate, caring-natured people to be a part of the disciple that worship and adore and put them on high pedestals. So it's those broken-hearted, kind souls that often come to me, who are baffled as to why loving somebody could cause them so many problems," she said. Corroborating a study from the University of Buffalo in 2015 that analysed 31 years of data of narcissism research and found that men were more narcissistic than women in most areas, Taverner said most of the victims she met were women.

My experience isn't unique. In the UK we're coming to understand the breadth of emotional abuse, of which narcissism is a key component. As I write this, the case of Sally Challen is going through an appeals process – Sally killed her husband after what her two sons said was a lifelong campaign of psychological abuse waged by their father through his coercive controlling behaviour. She was convicted of murder in 2011 and is now serving an 18-year sentence, but her appeal might see her conviction reduced to manslaughter thanks to a new law recognising coercive control as a crime.

A common understanding of narcissism can be more useful than the medical terms in which it's often expressed. Taverner says: "The medical model can be particularly unhelpful when for me I'm looking at the individual holistically from a biopsychosocial model in terms of influence, class, race." She adds that acknowledging someone in your life is a narcissist means taking a hard look at yourself and why you ended up dating them. "What does that mean for you as an individual? Because if your partner is a narcissist, you're more likely to attract that type of individual again," she explained.

While the onus to change shouldn't be on the survivor of a wrongdoing, perhaps victims of a less vicious type of narcissism need to be introspective about our own behaviour. "What do you need to learn to protect your niceness, to protect your kindness and who you are?" Taverner said.

For women, so often socialised to be empaths, it's about building up our defences and knowing when to leave a situation in which you're being used.

THE BEAUTY OF SITTING STILL

Tahmina Begum

Tahmina Begum is a freelance journalist and the editor of XXY Magazine. As a second generation south Asian woman, she finds the concept of comfort zones complicated. How to level the expectations of immigrant parents who have made sacrifices to build a better life, with the need to carve out time of your own?

To say you're comfortable – and I don't just mean in your chair – is often seen as unambitious and lazy, especially in a time where meetings are planned six weeks in advance and self-care is slotted in on a Sunday.

For a long time, watching peers sway in and out of their comfort zones has been something I've envied. How do I get there? Where can I find my comfort zone? When will I learn to be content? To me, having a comfort zone has rarely meant being complacent. If anything, it has always detailed a level of privilege.

Writers are often told their craft is like wine: it gets better with age and comes alive when drunk with lived stories around the table. But I've always felt as though a timer has been set for me. As a second generation south Asian woman, you're expected to marry and put your own needs second as soon as you have worked for a few years. In other words, you rarely reach a point where you can be comfortable; you're too busy trying to squeeze a career between the numbers 20 and 30.

Last year I visited seven places around the world, some for work, some for pleasure. The need to taste peculiar fruits and breathe air that made both my mind and body feel sticky was questioned by my parents, who saw this age – my mid-20s – as a time to prepare for future security. A crucial time to work hard. They couldn't understand my need for a break.

This kind of pressure isn't anything new. When you're black or brown, you're used to your needs being met in a DIY fashion. Take my parents, for example, who have lifted themselves out of poverty. For them, the notion of contentment – of taking a moment just for themselves – is alien. Suffering and overwork have been intrinsic to their identity for too long.

To be a child of an immigrant is to be forever attempting to match the sacrifices your parents made. It's difficult not to compare what hard work looked like in the traditional sense with the life I'm trying to build now: appointments taken in members' clubs and events furthering my platform and voice.

There's a feeling of owing your parents financial and emotional stability, which they were not afforded. A pressure to do something that involves 'working with your brains so you don't have to work with your back', as my Baba would say.

And yet the problem with chasing the next big thing on your to-do list – of always feeling like you have to push yourself, for yourself and those who came before you – is that you don't get to know who you are when you stay still. Who are you without the stress? What does your day look like when your mind is not running from one task to another? It's a question that's more relevant now that ever.

With more and more people working in their own way – we're all aware of the rise of freelance culture and the trend of maintaining a side-hustle alongside an already multi-faceted career – our business and pleasure time as well as our 'on' and 'off' buttons have become blurred.

The glamourisation of being booked and busy means we say phrases such as 'I can sleep when I'm dead' or 'you only live once'. It puts pressure on constantly living your best life. Whether that's having numerous weekend plans, trying to learn a new hobby (in case you don't sound interesting enough at social gatherings) or going for a job that sounds like a good opportunity but may not be good for you.

But what I've learned most from growing into myself, is that there's a beauty in staying still. There's a power in knowing that discomfort isn't a tally system: you don't need to reach the same level as those before you, or those around you, to know you've worked hard. You don't have to struggle in order to justify having good things in life.

There's a deep bond with yourself when you learn to let things go, even the things you prayed for and thought you wanted. It can be healing to know pain and sacrifice don't have to be inherited or generational, and that your comfort can ebb and flow. Like most things, it should. I find it's only when you're extremely comfortable or uncomfortable for long stretches of time that you feel an imbalance, and you eventually burn out.

There's a comfort in knowing the difference between push and pull – and when you just need to be.

AFTER WORD

THE MAGIC OF SISTERHOOD

Brita Fernandez Schmidt

Brita Fernandez Schmidt is the executive director of Women for Women International UK. Having worked at the organisation for 10 years, she has witnessed first-hand the powerful effects of women pushing out of their comfort zones together. She reflects on sisterhood here.

You know when something doesn't feel comfortable. You can feel it in your gut. Your heart beats a bit faster. Your body gives you all the clues that something that doesn't feel natural, or safe. You're contemplating leaving your comfort zone. And then you do, and you are so aware of that fear sitting on your shoulder, with your inner voice saying: 'Are you crazy? You know this is going to go wrong. Why are you doing this? Stop now!' And then you do it anyway. You find your way through the uncomfortableness because somehow you know that not doing it could be worse.

I had always wondered why I sought out opportunities that were going to make me feel uncomfortable, until I read a book called Feel the Fear and Do It Anyway by Susan Jeffers. It describes how you can make your world bigger by doing things that scare you. That part made sense to me, but what was revolutionary was the idea that not going outside your comfort zone doesn't just mean your world won't get bigger, but that your world will actively shrink. Now, I welcome the feeling of going out of my comfort zone as an old friend who wants to help me grow.

The notion of comfort zones is closely linked to the expectations we grow up with. We're labelled, and then we live up to those labels. I, for example, have always been labelled passionate. It can of course be taken as a compliment, but it can also be twisted into something negative, as a means of defining what I'm not: not mature enough, not professional enough. It's the reason that now, being asked to give an academic lecture fills me with far greater fear than being asked to be an inspiring after-dinner speaker. (Though who's to say academic lectures can't be filled with passion?) Once you start to unravel those labels and the assumptions that go with them, you quickly realise how limiting they are.

Going outside our comfort zones is therefore a fundamentally rebellious act. It's about rejecting the labels and boxes into which we've been placed. The 'comfort' in comfort zone is to do with what we know; with that which is familiar. And as we leave our comfort zones and embrace ourselves fully, we open up and make ourselves vulnerable to the possibility of failure – only it never is failure, it's just an experience.

In the act of opening up, we allow connection to flourish. This connection is exactly what I felt as I read the amazing contributions in this collection. The openness in the writers' words – in their feelings and reflections – allows us to connect deeply with them, creating a strong sense of sisterhood.

Over the past 10 years I have met so many incredible women through our programmes. Women who have experienced trauma, violence and loss. Women who have no access to support, who don't know how to earn an income, or how to make their voices heard. I've seen how these women have gathered strength within themselves to trust that change is possible. They've made their way to our training centres or to the places where we enrol new participants, journeys that often involve getting permission from male relatives and spending hours travelling. They felt the fear, and they did it anyway.

A few years ago in Bosnia, I met two remarkable women. They were tall, strong, confident. They looked like sisters, and there was a bond between them in the way they laughed together, spoke together, listened to each other, quietly and unconditionally supporting each other. They were graduates from the Women for Women International programme and they stood out in the group of women I'd come to visit. I went over with a translator to talk to them. They told me they'd become friends through the programme. They'd lived in the same village but had never met until they both enrolled. Together they embarked on learning new skills, and through that journey discovered their vast potential. They both decided to grow medicinal herbs and learn how to use them to make herbal remedies. They created their own business, selling their produce. By joining together in leaving their comfort zones, they created a bond of sisterhood.

These women are pioneers. They are heroines, who are brave and leaving their comfort zones every day. They are my inspiration. They are my sisters. When we trust ourselves and leave our comfort zones, we not only help ourselves to be all that we can be; we inspire others to do the same.

This book helps us remember the amazing potential we can discover when we leave our comfort zones, and how many sisters are right there with us. Each contribution is an act of sisterhood that says: you are more; you can do anything; you are not defined by your comfort zone or anything else.

Only you get to decide who you are.

A note from the publisher –

At Jigsaw, we design and make clothes – not books. We find the best mills, we source the best fabrics and we design in-house, in south west London. We create clothes that women want to wear now, next year, for decades – and then pass on.

But we know that the women who wear Jigsaw express themselves beyond clothes. They're opinionated, informed, funny. They're unafraid to step out of their comfort zones. So when Sonder & Tell approached us with the idea for this book, we knew instantly that we wanted to be the publisher.

We have taken the same uncompromising approach to publishing as we do to fashion. And we've taken a risk in doing this, but the work couldn't have been more rewarding, and that's even before (at the time of writing) the book going on sale. When we learnt about the work of Women For Women International – and the stories from the women on its training programmes – we wanted all proceeds from Comfort Zones to go to them. So when you buy a copy of this book from our stores or website, you can be confident that the full £9.99 goes towards the work of this brilliant charity.

We hope you enjoy reading the stories as much as we loved publishing them.

JIGSAW